Finding Your Identity

Letting God Write Your Unique Story

Oscar Twikala

Finding Your Identity
Copyright © 2018 by Oscar Twikala

Photo Credit: "Red Umbrella in Storm" by Kevin Carden (Adobe Stock)
Cover Design: Dana Susan Beasley (www.angelarts.biz)

ISBN-13: 978-1720913535

ISBN-10: 1720913536

Dedication

I dedicate this book to: those who have gotten lost due to an event in your life and the good politicians who are out there trying to make a change, to men of God who are genuinely serving God and loving his people, to my brothers and sisters in Christ who need a little encouragement, to the co-worker who pushed me to write this book, to those out there in need of a parent, to those who have lost hope because life has been harsh to them, to my Mom and Dad for all of their support and love for me...I love them dearly, to those who have been abused, to those who believe we are one and are fighting for diversity and against racism, to those who have felt that religion has hurt them, to those who have said no to money and showed integrity instead....to the United States for you are the mother of all nations, to my pastor and his wife for all of their spiritual support, and to the east of the DRC—there is hope and to my assistant, for all her support and for making my job easier.

Table of Contents

Foreword by Tammie Polk

I met Oscar through a high school friend's mother and took interest in his project immediately! Why? It's because I am just like him. I was one who had a tough time finding their identity. I had things going for me and odds stacked against me at the same time.

I was raised in a Christian home with two parents, yet I witnessed abuse, was a victim of molestation at the hands of my brothers, dealt with the sting of divorce, entered the world of being raised by a single mother who never graduated high school and lived with a man who refused to marry her for more than twenty years, and watched my father have several relationships after he and my mother split.

I had to fight for my identity because I was determined to not have my mother's life. I had people to speak things over my life, much like Oscar did, that shaped my experiences. Yet, as I grew older, God began to show me that He truly has the last word! I lived past twenty-nine. I am married with three girls. I am an entrepreneur who has written twenty-two books and helps others do the same.

Along the way, I have loved, lost, and battled regret. My mother died. My relationship with my father became strained. My relationship with my brothers became nonexistent. Yet and still, my relationship with Christ has kept me going!

It is my hope and prayer that you will both see and understand Oscar's heart in what he will share in the pages to come. I will warn you—this will not be an easy read…it wasn't for me. Like him, I am the voice of one who has overcome through the power of God…may you go in His strength and do the same.

Introduction

What I have against you is that you have allowed so many people to treat you less than your real value. This is a reality of not only people whom I can discuss, but also, sometimes this is what the Lord has taught me before, and that's what I see or feel that God is telling us today.

This is not just words but it a statement from God to His children who have lost their identity, which is a very important thing. We do not know how much we are worth because we have allowed our spouses, friends, circumstances, and situations to devalue who we are.

This can be anything. Let us just call this the Enemy. We are still experiencing the effect of what happened long ago. In many ways, we have allowed the Enemy to steal and destroy our identity! This can sound harsh to someone who has been raped or abused who would say, "Hey, I didn't do anything. It just happened". I am referring to how you reacted to the situations that destroyed your identity.

In the Genesis stories, we have those who we call Mother and Father, yet we also have questions. Why did they fall? Why did they sin? I can hear God saying to them, "You have allowed the Enemy to treat you less than your real value."

Identity crisis is a part of our story. We are all in the same place. That is where we were when the Enemy broke our hearts, sold us into slavery, abused and raped us, and took away what was most important to us. That is the place of crisis—where we lost control. We lost hope. We have allowed so many people to treat us this way. I hope that, through this book, the Lord will open your eyes. You are a child of God, the King of the universe. I hope that the Lord will find you as He found me.

Let us talk about identity. As we know, this world says that our identity is important. I am from the capital city Kinshasa in the Democratic Republic of Congo. In my country, and even in Kinshasa, there are things that do not require showing an ID. For major things, such as buying a house, traveling, and getting a marriage license, you will need an ID, but I remember renting a house without having to prove my identity. The owner took me at my word and rented me the house. It is crazy. I have been in the Congo my whole life and do not remember ever having to prove my identity.

Being in a country like America, identity is very important. We need IDs for everything. When I came here, I realized how important identity is. Our very identity is critical. Let us just think about the future which is really happening now: microchips and digital IDs. Identity will be crucial to everything. Social security numbers and drivers' licenses will soon not be enough to prove your identity. Identity will be all-important, not just in America and in Congo, but throughout the entire world. Today in America, the economic and governmental system does not care where you come from as long as you can prove your identity with an SSN. When applying for a job, buying a house, buying a phone, proving residency, with everything, you must prove your identity.

For example, those who are labeled as criminals and thieves are stuck because of the label put on them, which prevents them from moving forward. The world teaches us— nature teaches us—who we are by the labels put on us.

Let us put this into the context of a woman who has lost her identity because she

10

had been raped or had something tragic that happened in her past. In a way, she is in the same place as a criminal who is stuck in that place from which she cannot move forward. She wants to get married and have a family, but she is stuck because the past is pulling her back.

Consider someone who lived his whole life without a mother or father or a person and is now a criminal with a bad record. He is stuck in a moment because of a situation that happened in the past. He wants to move forward but he cannot move forward.

I have heard a lot about people who have poor credit. They go to an institution or bank to clean off their past and then people can trust them again. In the process, they give you baby steps such as with taking a small loan, and from that point on, you can move forward. We have all been there. We could not move forward. We needed help. I needed help. In some areas, I still need help, and I am not ashamed of it and have nothing to feel bad about.

I believe that, through this book, we can have that moment of cleaning and, by taking baby steps, we can get to a bright future, to a good future. I hope that we will be critical thinkers and ask questions.

I have always been a thinker. At the age of 6, I asked questions about the universe, such as where do we came from, yet I found no answer. Before I go into details, I will talk about the confusion I have myself about my own identity. I have tried to identify myself in many ways and through many circumstances and situations in my life—whether by relationships, religion, or power. Other people try to identify themselves by ethnicity, race, and relationships. In this book, I will talk in more detail about myself and other people I have interacted with.

CHAPTER 1 THE BEGINNING

I understand that many people are trying to find their way—their identity. Freedom was brief. What happened in the Garden can also be a reality today. When the Devil came to Eve, his goal was to get her to trade her identity. He stole Adam and Eve's identity. He knew who they were, but they didn't know who they were. What was the result? He bought it at a very cheap price.

When you read that story, you must understand that it is not just another story. This is something that happened to Adam and Eve and you can find yourself in their shoes. Look at it this way: there's something that you have traded with the Enemy. There is something that he has stolen from you because you were ignorant and you didn't know who you were. He'll come and tell you anything to make you trade your identity.

When most people read this account in Genesis Chapter 3, they see it as just another tragic story, but it is not. The Enemy played Eve. Adam and Eve had everything. When I am talking about everything, I am not talking about the trees and the fruit or the riches of the Garden, but a relationship with the Creator. The Enemy told them that they needed more. He tells us the same thing today—that we need more—and that is the reason you do not have joy. You believe that you need more than this job, more than this house. That's the reason we kill each other—we need more.   The reason we cheat on one another is that we believe we need more. We lie to one another because we want more. That is a sad reality, but it is true.

The Enemy will come and tell you anything. It can be smoking. I am not trying to put anyone down, by any means. What I am saying is that he will come and say, "Take this cigarette. You're stressed. You have a lot going on. Relax with this cigarette." And the result? You get to the point that you're trading your health.

When people are depressed, the Enemy will tell them, "You should drink more," and then, by doing so, you may start having unprotected sex, and the result may be pregnancy or sickness –all because you didn't know who you were! "Try to do this, and you'll feel better." No! No! So that's the crisis of identity—Crisis!

There are so many going through crisis. The girl who has been raped or abused by her father doesn't see any value in herself because he has stolen her value by force. You need to take it back! You need to have it back! The thing is you see yourself as a prisoner because you don't have an identity. It's hard for you to move forward in life.

You've lost your identity because of an abusive boyfriend who only used you for his pleasure. He had sex with you and then left you for another girl. As a result, you start seeing yourself according to what he is saying that this is what you're worth. The result? You start to think, "Well, maybe I deserve this. I am not pretty enough." You have lost your identity.

Then, we have this group of people who say "Yeah, I've been hurt. That's why I am who I am." You don't have to be who you are based on what happened to you. I understand what happened is unfair. They have raped you. They have abused you. They have done this to you and that's been your experience. Everyone else has their own experience and I know yours might be worse. It might be hard, but, do not lock yourself away due to that experience. You cannot value yourself according to the person who abused you and says that you are not worth anything. You have to allow yourself to move forward. When we lock ourselves away, we look back and still have that picture in our minds: "This is what they have done to us. This is what happened to us". You're still there! But how about you leave the moment? How about if you leave that behind?

The first step is not to see everybody else just like the person who hurt you. This is a different person. You cannot even enjoy the relationship that you are in right now because you cannot leave the moment and are still stuck in the past. It still affects you. Know who you are and know that your identity is not in the past.

Let's talk about those in slavery. People believe that they will always be slaves. No—that's just an experience. Several people have experienced terrible things in the past. Don't live in the past! Live in the present and build up the future for the people who will come after you. Be a warrior, fight against what happened to you, and defend those who have had been caught up

16

in slavery. Don't beat up yourself and cry over what happened to you. Yes, it is a terrible experience, but how bad do you think it is? If it's bad, would you ignore it when it happens to someone else? If not, then fight for and defend others. When you find yourself, help others to find themselves. That's the next step. The first step is to find yourself—find your identity. Once you find your identity, help others to find their identity, as well.

You're not who you choose to be, either. A cell phone cannot choose to be a cell phone. According to the one who created it, it is a cell phone. A cell phone cannot wake up one morning and say, "Well, I want to be a computer." No, it doesn't work that way. You were made to make phone calls. A car cannot say, "I don't want to be a car anymore. I choose to be a plane." It doesn't work that way. You were created to be a car.

This choice is something that the Enemy has stolen from you because you are ignorant, and you do not know who you are. In some things, you are trading your health to feel good and don't see that the devil is lying to you. What you really end up getting is death, and not only physically. He lies about everything—sex, drugs—whatever will make you feel better. You get to the point where you are trading your health for death and trading your identity at the cheapest price. You are worth more than that. We did not know what we had in the Garden...nor what we lost.

We are having an identity crisis. There will be some sort of crisis. A woman whose father is Black and whose mother is White will have a conflict of her identity. It becomes hard for us to define ourselves by race, gender, and ethnicity. If she thinks that she can ignore the Black side, it will pull her back down. Both sides are part of her identity. Embrace both sides! I interviewed a young Black American who identifies himself as Black, yet he has a parent who is Mexican. He grew up in a Black community and wanted to connect to his Mexican side, but there was a language barrier. Now, he is learning Spanish!

I know that America was born out of religious freedom and the Bible. The Bible was the foundation of everything and it was used to organize everything. Genesis 1:26a, 27 ESV says, "Then God said,

'Let us make man in our image, after our likeness'. So, God created man in his own image, in the image of God he created man; male and female he created them." God did not create Black or White. He created man. In humanity, there are many colors. Take a picture of the rainbow, make a collage of many people of different races, and take time to observe the beauty of the diversity of God. The more you embrace this diversity, then the more you will be able to enjoy it. The more you fight against diversity, the more you will hurt yourself and others. If we understand this, then it will become easier for others to understand their identity.

If I know my identity, then I will not allow others to demean or devalue me. I will give you an example. Suppose a police officer pulls me over because he does not like my face. Is this right according to the law? If I hired a lawyer, he would tell me that the police officer does not have a right to pull you over because of the way I look. It does not make sense.

Our identity is not based on color. We are human beings—that is who we are. Your identity is hidden in the Creator. So, how can you

19

know your identity? By knowing and understanding your Creator. Suppose I am driving my car like a truck or a plane. If you do not drive it according to Honda's specifications, then there will be a crisis. The functions of the Honda are according to the designer, not according to how I think the car should be driven. I need to understand the car according to how that Honda designer made it.

In thinking about the origins of life, I have gained respect for the great thinkers who have shared their revolution. Georges Lemaitre, a Belgian priest, and physicist proposed the Big Bang theory that "the universe began from a single primordial atom[1]"

Here, I am presenting this alternate view of the origin of life. What I need you to understand is the way the Creator has created you. One thing that I agree with is that human life had a beginning. What Lemaitre refers to as the "Big Bang," you will find in Genesis 1. You need to accept that you were created. If you do not know your origin, then you will not know where you will be going. What is your legacy? You

---

[1] ("The Origins of the Universe." *National Geographic*, www.nationalgeographic.com/science/space/universe/origins-of-the-universe/. Par. 6. Accessed 7 March 2018).

need to discover what is the mind of the Creator and what His plan is for you. I know that, for my Honda Civic, I have to use a certain grade of gas and change the oil every three thousand miles. That is the plan the creator had for my car. When you read the Book of Genesis, you will see that Adam did not do what the Creator planned. He went his own way and created a path of chaos.

Furthermore, I agree with Lemaitre in that there was an origin from which things began. What he calls an atom, I call Adam. In the biblical account, there is a Creator making everything happen. If you believe in your own theory, are you in peace? Are you going the way you want to go?

Many people are rich and seem to have everything. Michael Jackson is one example and yet, he was not at peace. I am not talking about wealthy people who donate their money to help others, build schools, or start industries to create opportunities for people within a community.

The problem is not what you have—you need to know who you are on the inside. People like him have millions of dollars, yet the money will not bring them peace. People were not created for riches.

Consider Adam in the Garden of Eden. Was Adam created for Eden, or was Eden created for Adam? We were not created for materials. We live like we have been created, but the materials were created for us, for our needs.

The identities of some are hidden in their money and they soon became controlled by it. In Congo, you will see wealthy politicians and businessmen buy expensive cars and clothes, live extravagantly, fly first class, and have the only beautiful home in their community. The religious leaders live around people who are poor. These "men of God" drive around in fancy cars while their church members are living in poverty. These rich and powerful people still want to fill a void.

Why would they use something like drugs when they have everything? They are preaching about Jesus—the One Who had all the riches and power in the universe—but lived a simple life. He did not own a home. He could have lived better than King Solomon but chose to live a humble life. In Matthew 8:20, He said this to a wealthy scribe, "Foxes have holes, and birds of the air have nests, but the Son of Man has nowhere to lay His head". Jesus's definition of being rich is developing people—He will always be about people.

As we continue in this book, we will explore more questions of identity—some rhetorical and some we will try to answer together. My hope is that, through this journey, you will find yourself, get to know who you are, and that you will come out of your identity crisis if you are in one.

CHAPTER 2 MY CRISIS

My family was spiritual, not necessarily Christian, but followed the same values. I went to a Catholic school, where I went to mass and loved the priest and the nuns. They were nice and they seemed so holy in their white robes. The white robes played with my mind.

I was trying to find myself. I was a very lonely child. The Catholic church was there for me and I became attached to it and the Virgin Mary. They taught me about Mother Mary and I fell in love with her. At mass, they would talk to her and pray to her.

I was a kid in primary school needed a mother. I was living with my stepmother, but she was not my mother. She was not there as a mother for me. I would be on the balcony, thinking about my real mother. My father said that men were soldiers and we did not need a mother. He told me that, when you sign up to be a soldier, they will give you a gun and tell you to kill your mother and father—that's how it was under Mobutu's regime. In my heart, I thought that I could never become a soldier. I was thinking, "I love you, Dad. I don't think I could ever do that."

My Dad's statement was very harsh, but Jesus also had the same harsh statements. In Luke 14:26 ESV, He says, "If anyone comes to me and does not hate his own father and mother and wife and children and brothers and sisters, yes, and even his own life, he cannot be my disciple". If I would have heard these words then, I would think that he was harsh.

I was a child and I wanted my mother, but I couldn't ask my father for anything more. He never explained why my stepbrother was living with his mother, when he was also supposed to be a soldier, according to what my father said. So, I held on to Mary and was on the balcony talking to her. Sometimes, I talked to Jesus, but I needed a mother. I used to sing songs to her in Lingala, one of the languages in Kinshasa. That was me trying to find my identity through religion.

I did not know the meaning of religion. I was just a boy trying to figure out who I was. I was a thinker and thought a lot at that time. Growing up in that faith, I had questions come to mind, but they did not bother me enough to ask them. One day something happened that changed that. I was around nine or ten years old and in primary school. My classmates started going to the bathroom one by one. I thought to myself, why were they going to the bathroom so much? Then it became my deskmate's turn. He went and came back and said, "Something's going on!" One of the sisters was having sex in the office. That office had a mail slot in the door, so the kids would peak through there. When it was my turn, I did not question it. I said to myself, okay, I'll go. It changed me. It was a shock. I was so mad, and I told myself no one else would see this! I kicked the door and then no one had any more to see. That was a shift in my identity. Before that turning point, I had never questioned the priest and the nuns. I took them at their word. I started to ask a lot of questions about religion. I questioned why we had rosaries. I was told that I had a Heavenly Father, but with my earthly father, I did not need a rosary. I did not accept and cling to the rosary as my friends did. As a boy, I believed that all the sisters were the same. Now, I know that the sisters are humans like everyone else and they make mistakes.

I know that there are good sisters and I met one at the Chiara Center Franciscan

Place of Spirituality. During the valuable time with Sister McQueen, the thing that I learned from her was silence. She said that a lot of people are afraid of silence because it will take them to a place of solitude and they don't want to feel lonely. She said that it is not always a bad place because in silence you can hear yourself, hear God, or hear what is going on around you.

I remember going there at a time in my life when I had a lot on my mind and felt heavy spiritually, but I did not know what I needed. I did not know that it was a silent retreat. I was looking for my own private retreat, but I went to Sister McQueen's retreat. The only thing, at that time, was I had to remain silent. I went to breakfast and dinner without talking to anyone. Yes, it seemed awkward.

I went to the park at the retreat center, intending to pray, and I heard a voice tell me, "Oscar, remain silent." I was determined to pray, but I kept hearing that voice telling me to remain silent. As soon as I obeyed, I was able to hear the birds singing with their beautiful voices, could feel the wind caressing my face, and was connected to the nature around me.

As a child, my mother introduced me to her religion. She was Christian and there was a lot of intercessory prayer at her church. I had the Catholic faith in school, Christianity with my biological mother, and Mormonism with my dad and stepmom. I tried to find myself among these three religions. I tried to find myself through relationship. These three religions and relationships pulled me in three different directions.

My need for my mother made things hard because I was still trying to find myself. Religion was one of those things to help me find it, but at first, it did not make sense. When I was with my mother, I would feel the love, connection, and the peace that I wanted. This only lasted for a brief time and then I would be taken back to my dad and my stepmom. I had a shock with the Catholic church and, with Mormonism, how my stepmother treated me affected me greatly.

She abused me, but I could not tell my father. I carried all of that chaos inside. My stepmother tore me down and said negative things about my mother. I kept it to myself. I am not talking bad about her, but about what I experienced. My father wanted me with him, but my stepmother wanted me to leave the house, many times late at night. I remember one night when this happened, I had to wait for my Dad to come back home. It was dark and I was scared, sitting on the street and praying and that he would come home soon. Yet, I knew that my father often came home late. I wondered if he would even come home at all. Through this and many other experiences, I have learned how to wait.

I had to wait for the gatekeeper to open the gate for my father and then, I would sneak in after him and watch him go up one set of stairs while I would take the other. When my father went to his room and changed clothes, I went back to my room and got back into bed, knowing that my father would come and check on me. Once my dad was in the house, I finally felt safe. My stepmother and I knew what really happened, but I would say nothing to avoid conflict between my stepmom and dad. I kept the burden to myself.

Then, one night, I had a dream one night about a loving man who I was playing with in our empty swimming pool. He was loving and kind and I felt like I was the happiest child ever. Soon, the man said that he had to go. I told him no, I am going with you. He said it wasn't time yet. When I woke up, I was so sad.

Another time, I remember being sick and in the hospital. I was never afraid to die. In fact, I told him that I was going to die. My father became angry and yelled, "Never speak like that again! No, you're not going to die!" I always knew that there was something greater and better than life here on earth, because I kept having that image of the man who left.

I wanted to join him. I always knew that I wanted to be with him. This brought on deep depression, along with these negative things my stepmom said about me. My stepmother would always just put me down. When people do that, you lose confidence and have low self-esteem. That's where I was. When I went to my mother's house, I received love and felt alive. When I returned to my father's house, the routine would be the same. It affected my grades. I would have good grades and then they would just drop. I considered myself an intelligent person, but this brought me low—to a person who I was not. Even now that I am writing this book, I would never have believed that I could   be that person.

30

I believed everything that my stepmother said about me. I believed that I was stupid. I believed that I was dumb. I always had this thought I would be the servant to her children in the back of my mind. I thought I was a fun-loving happy child in love with people and my family. Then things started to change. My mom gave me the love I wanted until I had to lose her. I had so much in my heart that I wanted to give to others. When I lost her, and I still had so much love to give, I did not know what to do. I had too much love in me, and I thought my father would be too overwhelmed. I wanted to give my father the love that I had once given to my mother, but I knew it was too much.

I wanted to give and receive great love, so I tried with my best friend and my girlfriend. It did not last long. She told me that that I had too much love to give and that she was not my mother. Then I thought that my best friend would accept and receive this love I had to give, but he betrayed me by going with my girlfriend. All of this chaos—all of this hurt—gave birth to a different person. Soon, I became violent, started drinking, and started going from one girlfriend to another. How did I know that was not the person who I was? I felt like a fish out of water. I felt like something was missing. When I was with my friends, I felt like something was missing. Everything that I did with my friends, I would do to the extreme because I was driven by all the hurt that had built up by all the things that had happened. I lost my identity.

Was I really that person? Or, was I still that lovely little boy who loved and was ready to love? I shifted to this other person. It could happen to anyone. You may have experienced this, too. If you know me now, then you would not expect that I was that other person. You would wonder where this behavior came from. I don't believe that people are born to be criminals, prostitutes, etc. You become who you are based on your experiences on what you have seen and what you have heard.

Recently, I have been helping a father of two little girls who has been in prison. When I met him, I started discipling him and helped him find a job. I thought things were working for him, so I started trusting him more. One day, he came to me and said that he needed a car for work. I got him a car in my name, but he did not make the payments, and I was stuck paying this $11,000 bill. I kept going back to him and I wanted to help him work this out. This loan had already gone to the creditors and I knew that he could not make the payment. I am not going to lie. That hurt!

Even a person like him has a good person inside of him. So, you tell me. Does someone like him deserve a second chance? Do you want to pause and ask why he behaves this way? Because of the person that I am now, it can be a conflict. Or was it another lesson for me to learn how to love? One thing is for sure: people act that way because of the crisis in the world. We call them names and we label them. They need our help. Even through all of this, my prayer was for my own heart. I love him. I forgive him. Does he deserve it? No, but this is my nature. This is my identity.

You see, I am at the point now where it doesn't take a lot to lose it. If I allow the anger to take over, then my identity is gone. If his soul is valuable, then what is it worth? Is it worth more than $11,000? These questions were on my mind. Is there any bank out there that will trust me again? Then I am like, no, my identity lies in something greater and in someone greater. I found it in forgiveness. That is how I kept my identity.

As I looked back at my school years, I realize that the chaos I experienced at home—and how I reacted to it—making noise, and not focusing caused the teacher to become mad. I became good at bringing the chaos into the classroom. It caused me to misbehave and I was good at it. I would make a mess or make noise because my friends liked it when I acted out, but my teacher did not. I needed to be disciplined.

Then one day—I do not remember exactly what I did—I got on my teacher's last nerve. I was making a mess and he told me that he did not know what to do with me. He said that he did not know what he would do if he laid a hand on me. So, he took me to the principal's office. He told me that he was supposed to whip me...to kick my butt. But what that man did, I will never forget. It is fresh in my mind. What the principal did that day, I will never forget. If on that day, he had used a ruler or a stick, then probably I would have gone back to class and back to my old behavior. But what that man did that I will never forget.

He gave me an identity. He said that face and my behavior did not match. He said my face looked innocent. He described who I really was. I realized that this is who I am and this is what my principal did for me. That is what we need to do for people when they mess up, misbehave and are losing their minds, and when they go crazy. You must remind them who they really are.

So, this man told me, "Your behavior and your face do not match. You look like a lamb. Go back to class and do not repeat whatever you did." When I left that room, I was shocked. Who talks like that? I do not even know if that man was a Christian, but who talks like that! That was the voice of God coming through that man! It is the same thing that Jesus said to the adulterous woman in John 8:10-11 NASB, "'Woman, where are they? Did no one condemn you?' She said, 'No one, Lord.' And Jesus said, 'I do not condemn you, either. Go. From now on sin no more."

Yes, I was condemned by the teacher, but the principal said, "Go back to class." The principal was not condemning me. He made me realize who I am. And just like Jesus said, "Go. From now on sin no more." So, do we do the same thing with people in our lives? Are you the one who helps other people get saved or are you the one who condemns? This is what we all should do. Those old behaviors were not my true identity and were based on the pressures of my home life. I was still that innocent kid, but I had lost my identity.

A new chapter of my life began when I became a teenager. I met new friends and was introduced to drinking, partying, and girls. These things caused fights and competitions with other guys at the parties, either with how we dressed or the cars we drove. I was hurting other people, hurting inside, and had my butt kicked many times, too. I went from that innocent kid to a hooligan.

The things I saw and heard influenced my identity. Even more, I could still hear my stepmother's voice, "You will not succeed. You are nothing. You will be the servant of my children," and all the other horrible things that she said to me about my mother. The people in my life and the environment I grew up in created this new me. Deep in my heart, I knew that I was still searching for who I was and for my own identity. I share my experience to show you and explain how people get to the place where they are.

It doesn't just happen overnight. The things that they go through hurt them. They are trying to defend themselves, but in the wrong ways. That is what I call a crisis. The pain directs the behavior. The pain has taken ownership of you and caused you to behave in certain ways. Many of us, when we see others behave a certain way, the first thing we do is we judge. We don't try to understand the real cause of the problem—the why, which is the most important thing to identify.

Think about the nice girls trapped in prostitution. You want to approach them and find out how they got there. Some got there because they were raped by their own fathers. They got mad and they lost their identity. They think that they have no value because if their own parent would rape them, then maybe that's what they're worth. So, they become prostitutes. Others grew up in a home where the mother or father was a drug addict, and I can go on and on....

People are where they are for so many reasons. The girl who was selling her body—she didn't want to—but she has no choice because she needed money to support herself. It's the condition she is in. She thinks that if she doesn't do this, it would be the end. She needs someone to be there and talk to her and show her the way. Jesus did it!

He didn't judge, instead, He interacted with the prostitutes, showed them the way, and people were shocked! "How could you talk with this person?" Let me ask you this. How many of us are afraid to interact with certain people because we afraid to shock other people? What will people think when I am talking to this prostitute, this drug addict, or this alcoholic. Jesus made a difference with one interaction. If you want to make a difference, interact with people, understand the struggle, and let God save them through you.

This is my story. I am putting it out there to explain how somebody can lose their way. This is how I went from a nice boy to a hooligan and, through religion, lost my way. Trying to find myself was not a painless process. How do you find yourself? How do you regain your identity once you have lost it? I am asking these questions with you and want us to search for the answer to identity together. We are living in a fallen world where some ideas about identity are skewed.

Growing up, my stepmother gave me tasks to do in the house. In our culture, women are in the kitchen, helping with cleaning, doing dishes, and so forth. On the other hand, men are outside, cleaning the car, mowing the yard, and things like that. What my stepmother was asking me to do was girls' duty—not to say that it was only girls' duties. In my culture, it was girls' duty. My stepmother and sisters would come and ask me to clean the house, do dishes, etc. I felt it was very disrespectful that, while my sisters were watching TV and enjoying themselves, I would be doing the cleaning. I would go ahead and do it—until I came to a point where I thought that, now I am a grownup, my stepmother cannot ask me to do things like that while my sisters were there.

One time, my older sister tried to force me to clean the house, but then I said no and pushed her. I started thinking that I have power now…that I'm in a position of power. A couple of times, I thought that I should face my stepmother, say no, and be disrespectful to her. I remember when she came and asked me to clean the house and do the dishes. I was so mad and I did not want to do it. I was thinking that this was it now and I will talk to her! But, thank God, before I did that, I went to talk to one of my aunts who was also living in my father's house. I told her that I was feeling very disrespected when my stepmother asked me to do things while my sisters were there or even sometimes when the maids were there. I was mad and said, "You know what?! I'm done! Now, I will go talk to her and finish this now with her!"

My aunt taught me something that day. She said, "Oscar, you know what? I will ask you one thing, and that is to do it. Go clean the house. Go do whatever she asks you to do." I'm like, "No! I am done! I am not going to do it! I am done with her!" But she taught me, "Oscar, someday you'll be in your own house and nobody will tell you what to do. Someday, you'll be at your own house and nobody will ask you to clean and stuff like that, so just do whatever she's asking you to do." The words that my aunt used that day convinced me, so I calmed down and went and I did it. If it weren't for her, I believe that day I was going to do something stupid. So, why am I sharing this? I was that young kid who felt that I was abused and asked to do extra work to make me feel less or powerless. So, for me, using power was going against her authority and fight her. She wasn't right—she was doing that to take advantage of me, make me feel bad, and make me feel that I am nothing. But, was fighting her the way to defend myself? Was playing that power game a way of defending myself?

Most times, we misunderstand power. For me, this was a huge misunderstanding of power. I wanted to defend myself and thought, "Now I'm a man and they cannot take advantage of me. I am not weak." I became violent and wanted to fight with that anger burning in my chest, but that wasn't the right way of doing things. That's not power.

The most powerful person in the history of humanity exercised His power by allowing people to mistreat treat Him to the point of suffering a painful death on a cross! He went on to save a lot of people after that. The most powerful person in the universe had been treated as the weakest.

There's a better way to defend ourselves without becoming violent. Martin Luther King, Jr. fought for human rights so that all people would be treated the same no matter the color of their skin. It would have been easy for him to raise up his own army to fight for human rights. It's the same with Nelson Mandela. Though he was innocent, he was imprisoned for twenty-seven years. When he was released, he could've raised an army to fight against the Whites who imprisoned him, yet he used another way—love. I learned to allow my heart to love instead of misusing power. I didn't need to fight wrong with anger. Yes, I had become a man and was able to fight back, but that only made it worse. I tried through relationships, religion, and violence and it didn't work.

So, what worked for me? I was born in love, ready to love and had so much love to give. It was easy for me to love my mother, who was the first person I saw when I opened my eyes. In my father's arms, I fell in love with him immediately. When my siblings sang over me, I fell in love with them. But, when I grew up, I asked things like, "How could a man love two women at the same time?" When my mom passed away, I went to my father, but he wouldn't receive all my love. Then, I gave all my love to a girlfriend, but she said that she was not my mother. I loved my best friend, but he betrayed me. I took my love and bottled it away. That was me trying to find myself—going from one place to another. Many people face this, yet cannot find what they are looking for.

CHAPTER 3 MONEY OR DIGNITY?

In this chapter, we will talk about people who have lost their identity or have sold their identity for money. My friend Ingrid dealt with this through what she experienced in Congo. Ingrid is one of those people who said no and refused to sell her identity for money. She, along with myself and others, have had to deal with corruption in the workplace and it was so easy to fall prey to temptations.

What we need to understand is that we don't become people who become addicted to money in an instant. It comes from a temptation—an offer made to you. One thing about temptation is that it always comes during times of weakness. It doesn't come when you are strong or in a position of power, but when you are vulnerable. One example is in Matthew chapter 4. It says Christ fasted for 40 days and nights. He was hungry, tired, and weak. Can you imagine Christ being in that position and then someone coming along and offering Him bread? He was in a position of weakness, but He didn't sell his identity.

The difference between Christ and Adam was that Adam sold his identity for one bite! Christ was starving, but never sold His identity for bread; however, Adam, who had everything, sold his for one bite. He sold his identity based on a lie and lost all humanity while Christ bought humanity back by giving away His identity.

That is the reality of people who have been treated as nothing. This is the message—a person tells you that you are worth nothing and offers you money to sleep with you. The worst-case scenario in Congo are the girls who offer themselves in exchange for lunch or a cell phone. I don't know if this is the reality in the US, but in Congo, it happened to many people.

People with power and money come to you, buy you shoes and cars, and then use you for their own pleasure. Men who are married keep their side girls. I would like to use the word "mistress," but it is not the right word because these men really devalue these girls who they keep for their own pleasure. On the other side, you will see rich older women get young men, buy them what they want, and then use them for their own pleasure.

Very young people, some are under the age of 16, sell their virginity because they accept that this is their identity. This didn't happen overnight. It comes from a place of weakness. For some, their dads were rich at one time and then lost everything. These young people are afraid to lose that lifestyle, so they sell their identity for shoes and fancy cars. A different group of people sell their identity because they want to have the same lifestyle that others have. These young people's families are poor and cannot afford cell phones, especially the newest version, that many of their peers have, so they sell their bodies by dating men old enough to be their father or their grandfather. They will seduce these girls, telling them that they want to be their girlfriend or that their marriages do not matter.

Sometimes, it is a need for a job because there aren't many jobs in Congo. Ladies, you may have had a good interview, and get hired for the job. What you don't know is that the boss likes you and wants to use you for sex. The women have bills to pay and families to support. For some, it becomes a life of prostitution. You see beautiful girls traveling with powerful men and men in the government and you think, 'Wow, she has a good life" when she has no identity.

While Ingrid was working on a project for her foundation that helps people who are born with sickle cell anemia, she was looking for business partners. She met a man who was interested in the project and he approached her. She told him that she was a Christian and that man claimed to be a Christian. Ingrid was excited about this. Later, things started to change. She no longer knew what the man was thinking. As they were approaching the signing of the contract, this married man made an indecent proposal. She didn't want to sell her identity in exchange for the contract, but she couldn't let go of the project that she had worked so hard for.

Even though this man came back to her and reminded her repeatedly how important this project is and that he would sign the contract, Ingrid said that she solely wanted to work with him on this project—not sleep with him. She continued to get texts and calls from this man. She felt she was being harassed by this man. She thought, "You are married, and you said you're a Christian! How can a man of God act like this?" The guy would drop it for a time and then come back, flattering her and reminding how important this project is. This man was doing all of this in order to have sex with her in exchange for signing the contract. Ingrid had the same response—that there is nothing more that they can do together apart from work. She could have easily slept with this guy and he would have signed the contract. Ingrid would have been able to start her foundation with a big check, but instead, she kept her dignity. This man would have lost all respect for her had she slept with him. Yes, she wanted to help people and didn't want to lose her work or the foundation, yet she was not willing to gain the entire world and lose her identity.

Another heartbreaking story is the 14-year-old girl in the neighborhood who was dating older men for money. She may sleep with her boyfriend's best friend for revenge, but she is just killing herself. These girls are selling and belittling themselves for nothing. I told a friend about this young girl and I wanted him to see her situation—cars dropping her off in the neighborhood several miles away from her house in the dark. I considered her age and knew I had to approach her situation delicately. She was caught in the lifestyle and I felt bad for her. I should have done something. I wanted to do something. While talking to her, I asked her some trick questions and realized that she knew what she was doing. She was young, had friends with fancy things, and wanted the new cell phone and clothes. This behavior didn't come out of nowhere—she saw the older girls that she looked up to in her neighborhood doing the same thing. She would see different girls, and even her own family members, selling themselves for money. It was a big deal, but she learned these things from the neighborhood.

What we need to understand is that we have a responsibility to the younger generation. I am guilty myself. The younger ones saw me partying with my guy friends and they thought we were cool. We were a bad influence even though the young girls thought we were cool. The younger boys would look up to us and ask us to talk to girls. I repented of that later because I realized that the younger generations saw us drinking, partying, and going to nightclubs. It broke my heart. You know, being a brother or father or mother, you need

49

to know you must show the younger people how to live right. The best way to teach honesty is to be honest yourself. To teach integrity, you must show integrity in your dealings with others. The way we live our lives matters to those who look up to us.

Furthermore, I was brokenhearted because this was the reality of the women living in my own neighborhood. These girls were selling their identity. Ladies, I need you to understand how much you are worth. You are special. You are beautiful. You are blessed. The responsibility is not only on the man, but it is part of your responsibility, too. Can you imagine someone trying to sell diamonds in a poor neighborhood in an open-air market along with cheap things? People would think he or she was crazy. They would think it's broken glass and not real diamonds. That is the wrong place to sell diamonds.

Growing up in Congo, we had plates for special guests. If a rich uncle or a business associate was coming for dinner, we would pull out the expensive plates and glasses. We were not allowed to use those expensive dishes for every day, otherwise, our family would say we are crazy. I wasn't allowed to use those plates to eat fufu, a staple food in Congo, on those plates or I would get into serious trouble! It would be the same thing if a young American child would try to eat his peanut butter and jelly sandwich on the special dishes during his afternoon snack.

Ladies and gentlemen, the way you present yourselves does matter. The way you present yourself is on you. Christ says that you are valuable, but you put yourself into bad positions where people will abuse you. In the Congo, there are young men who need a job so they will date a man who can give them the job, even though they themselves are not homosexual. These men will help the young men with their applications and the interview process— only to have these men offer them the job if they will sleep with them. I have a friend who has experienced that.

He applied for a job and everything went well. The boss told him he is a very good candidate and then said, "It would be a very good thing for you to sleep with me." My friend was desperate for a job, but he said no. Many people we knew were dating men to get their job. It happens all the time with businessmen and   politicians.

Then, there is the mother who dressed her daughter in provocative clothes. When she came home pregnant, her mother said, "Who did that to you?!" Well, the mother presented her daughter as an object for pleasure. I am not telling you that you can't get your identity back once it is lost. You can get it back. That's why I am telling you that you need a wake-up call.

These people are not worth it and will only use you for sex. The Enemy will tell you that you don't deserve to be happy, but don't settle for less. You don't have to marry someone who doesn't treat you with respect. You can't go to the mall, see something that costs a thousand dollars, and offer a dollar for it. The retailer would laugh at you and think that you were losing your mind. Don't allow people to bring you that low and devalue who you are. They don't deserve you. You are worth more than that, and the only person who can represent your value is you.

For some women, the boss will come to you, say that you're doing an excellent job, and tell you he can promote you. The problem with that is that, if you don't give your body to him, then you will lose the job. You can get another job, but once you lose your virginity, you cannot get it back. In this society, if you are sixteen years old and still a virgin, then you are made to feel like you are not cool. So-called friends will convince you to give it away. To the older generations, virginity was important and valuable. Girls today give it away just to be cool. No. It's part of your value. NO! You hold tremendous value. Girls today are losing their identities. If you hear testimonies from these older women, they will tell you that a woman would give her virginity to the guy she thought was the one. Then, their identity is shifted and they now have low self-esteem. She may not want to lose her boyfriend, so she is willing to go along with whatever he says. Girls, this is important—when someone loves you, he will protect and respect your values, not manipulate you in order to get something from you. If the guy truly loves you, then he will patient and honor you, not put pressure on you in order to get something in return.

Many women thought this person was the one and they gave so much of themselves—and even all they had—only to discover that they were empty when the person left them and now it's hard for them to move forward. That brings on the crisis and now, every man out there becomes the enemy. They should have said no and hung onto their value and their dignity when they saw that person was not the one. They should have waited.

God's command to the man is to love the woman. The man who loves you will value you and put your value first. They want you to rejoice and be happy, not manipulate you. Love will be the key—not what they give you, what they say, nor what they look like. How many people do you know-- that you went to high school with—who were popular and good-looking, but today have changed and not look the same? So, what's is the most important thing?

Another thing to keep in mind is time. Our generation rushes into love. If somebody says they love you, then watch him. Drag them to move slower and see if they are the same person. Don't give them what they want, but what they need. They need a friend, not a partner in bed—that's why they are called boyfriend and girlfriend. Don't rush into things. You need to see how they get mad. You will be surprised. Time is the key.

Money is another thing to watch out for. I Timothy 6:10 ESV says "For the love of money is the root of all kinds of evil which some reaching for it have been led astray and have pierced themselves many sorrows." Money itself is not a terrible thing—it is a good thing. The love of money becomes bad when it controls you, making you forget about people and become selfish. You start to think that the world revolves around you. People who want it will do anything for it and are willing to throw their respect, dignity, and integrity in the trash. It doesn't happen overnight, but comes step by step until, one day, you become very much in love with money.

In my job at the Department of Distribution, I did well and was promoted to be the Transportation Manager. When I got there and started working, I found there was a very corrupt system in place. I was working honestly and people resented me, but hid that from me. And then, the boss would say, "This was a bad month and I'm not able to pay you." My boss would then make me these promises and tell me I was a good worker. He would cause me to dream that we will have this and that.

Customers would come to me with a deal and ask if I could give them a lower price for use of the company truck and they would give me money in return—kickbacks. I would present a counteroffer and get extra money in return. I began stealing money from the company because the boss wouldn't pay me. My mind changed and became corrupt. I became just like my boss, the person that I didn't want to be. I told my boss that I couldn't work for him anymore and I left my job without a Plan B because I didn't want to be the person they wanted me to be.

What we need to understand is that dignity and integrity are part of your identity and you need to protect it. You can lose your job and your money, but don't lose yourself. I can come up with multiple examples with politics or in the church in the Congo. You see pastors who start a good work and have a good heart for the people, but, over time, they start loving money more than people. People are more valuable than money. You see some of these pastors lying to and manipulating people to get more money while their own people remained poor.

My father had a nice car gifted to him. Because his pastor said that the car had an evil spirit, my father gave his pastor the car. Later, I saw the pastor driving that car and I thought the spirits must be good to the pastor and only bother my father. I am not attacking this pastor, but like the Apostle Paul pointed out, there are wrong ways to do things.

You see stories like that and then you see young people going into ministry in Congo with the mindset of becoming rich and famous, not to serve people. If you become rich and famous, then praise God, but that isn't the goal. You will see pastors preaching on the Internet, but it is your responsibility to ask the Lord what He is calling you to do. Is this what He wants me to do, or do I just want to be known, rich and famous? I am not saying that all pastors in Congo are doing terrible things. I have seen faithful men of God serving in Congo. I remember thinking that I see all these people who are on top of the world, are famous, have money and they can do anything they want. What happens when you stand before God, and He acknowledges that you were a millionaire, everyone knew you, and you did well for yourself, but He says, "I never knew you". After a retreat in Texas, a friend and I were sitting on a bridge with water around us and I sat down and wrote the following poem that I named "Will you remember me?"

Will you remember me?

When men praise me and I feel that I have it all

When I am on the top of the world

When men build a statue in my honor

Will you remember me?

Would you—if I have all of power of the world, when people

die to see me, when the world is in my hands—will you

remember me?

When my name is on the cover of every magazine

When I am the subject of the news

Will you remember me?

When I have all of the riches of the world

When my playground is covered in diamonds and in gold

Will you remember me?

If that was the goal—to finish #1 or at the top of the list, good at everything, the best at everything, if that was the goal—to gain the whole world, yet lose my soul?

(If I would call this success, if I get to the point where I say that I have made it, will you still remember me?)

The truth is I would rather have no one know about me or remember me, but You.

So will you remember me?

My goal is to seek you.

My aim is to please you.

But yet that is not enough.

Your grace. That's all I want.

So please, remember me.

All I need to know in this life is that the love God has for me is not based on who I am, but in Who Christ is and what He did for me. That is where I find my peace. I have been thinking about comments that Jim Carrey has made. He went to an event to honor icons and, during an interview with a journalist, he said: "Jim

Carrey is just a character." Many people read that and don't understand what he means. For someone like Jim Carrey, who is famous and has a lot of money, that is very serious.

Recently, my friend Miriam and I went to encourage our friend Marty, who was depressed. This man was a millionaire who had everything in life that he could want. It shocked me when he said that he wished he were dead. He said that his family is gone and he's going through a divorce. But this man had everything! People came to him for money. He was going to give his wife 4 million dollars just to protect his family's legacy. I didn't even have a hundred dollars that day! I didn't even have two hundred dollars! At the time, I was very poor, yet I was encouraging this millionaire.

Money is not the most important thing in life—legacy is what matters. What you leave behind after you're gone is what matters. How many rich people have died and we never think about them anymore? Patrice Lumumba was the Prime Minister of Congo after the country gained its independence from Belgium. He didn't want to have anything to do with corruption or money. He died financially poor. Many people in Congo died richer than

Prime Minister Lumumba, yet he died spiritually richer than they were. Why am I saying this? He died with his dignity. He died for his people. More than fifty-seven years after Prime Minister was assassinated, look at the sad reality in Congo. The politicians think they are rich. All the money that the Congolese politicians have in banks in France, China, and Switzerland is helping the people of those countries, while their own people are poor and suffering. These corrupt politicians think that they are rich, but they have no dignity.

Every young person who wants to enter politics believes they'll become rich. That's not how it was. It used to be about serving the people. The younger generation thinks that they cannot change the corrupt system, so they may as well steal from their own people too. It's also a sad reality about the Church in the Congo. It's become political and all about money and power. People are looking for rest in the church, and instead, they find oppression. The pastors will make them feel bad and say that God needs their money, even if they don't have it. God doesn't need their money…He wants them. If God has your heart, then you will want to give

Him your money anyway. Our money is His money, and we are merely stewards of it.

One time I didn't pay my tithe and things were not going well in my life. I went to my pastor and said that I felt like I was stealing from God. The pastor told me to tithe three times my tithe to repair the damage! What pastors are called to do is what Jesus said to Peter in John 21:17 ESV, "He said to him the third time, "Simon, son of John, do you love me?" Peter was grieved because he said to him the third time, "Do you love me?" and he said to him, "Lord, you know everything; you know that I love you." Jesus said to him, "Feed my sheep."

I am the voice for those who feel oppressed and are afraid to talk about this subject. With the way we have presented this, we can't get feedback from the people. It's easy for a pastor, a man of God, to get greedy. We need to attack the sin of the men of God who have fallen into greed. We must respect them, but not fear them. We should only fear God. People fear that, if they say this about their pastor, then they'll die! No, give your pastor feedback for his wrongdoing! Pastors are just like our fathers. I used to talk to my Dad when I believed he was doing something wrong. I would say, "Well, Dad, why are you doing that? Maybe you shouldn't,' and he would have a chance to explain and say, "I am sorry, son, that you misunderstood". Just like with your pastors, they are human beings who make mistakes. They can say, "my son or daughter I am sorry" or they can say, "I am sorry that you misunderstood".

As I said earlier, money itself is not a terrible thing. It is the love of money that is the terrible thing. Money is needed to help the church and people in need. It is the mission of the church. Money is needed to facilitate the mission of the church. That is not bad. If a pastor is using the money to feed the sheep in the church and to help those in need, then that is fine. People don't want to hear about giving money, but it is for the work of the church and pastors shouldn't feel bad about asking for money to support the church. If the pastors' hearts are pure in asking for money to help the church and not so that they can use it for their own family or for things that they want, then that's good. We give for the love of God and for the love

63

of His people, but we are not forced to give. We don't give because we believe that we will burn in Hell. There is no such thing!

CHAPTER 4 KNOW YOUR VALUE

Any item we doubt the price of can end up in any hands. It can be in the hands of a rich or poor person. It's not wrong to be in a rich person's hands. It can go far on the streets, travel on the ground, or end up in the trash. I believe that all items need a price. It needs a value to be treated well. When we see a diamond or gold, what immediately comes to mind is that this is valuable. We care about how we touch it and carry it around. The moment that we know that it is ours, we keep it in a safe place. We hide it. We don't want anyone to know about the secret place except for the person we trust. So, know this, you have a lot of value.

You are worth more than a diamond. You are worth more than gold. You are worth more than anything material. I don't care about the price of diamonds and gold. You are valuable. So, why do you suffer? I'll tell you why. You need to know your own value. The reason you have let so many people treat you less than your real value is that you don't know who you are. Right now, you are saying to yourself, "You don't know my story and what I have gone through." You may say that I don't

65

care. This can sound harsh or judgmental. Yes, I agree and maybe I don't understand, but I do have my own experiences with this. Maybe yours is worse than mine. Maybe my experience is worse than yours. I am not trying to compare. I want you, together with me, to analyze things, others' stories and how it relates to ours. I will share about experiences that have affected me directly.

I remember walking home one day after work. I worked hard and had to walk to my aunt's apartment. While I was walking, I was complaining about how miserable my life was. I was complaining and complaining and complaining. Sometimes, I had to work late at night and come back early the next morning and work more. Sometimes, I had to walk at night and walk in the rain. One day, I was walking when the road was icy. There was a car at the stop light, while I was trying to cross the icy street. The driver of the car, a lady, was watching me as I fell. I felt like I was falling in slow motion! She saw me and, before I knew it, I hit the ground. The lady in the car was laughing at me and I laughed because it was funny. It was not funny to me, but I agreed that it was funny to her.

I complained about all of these things. As I got closer to the apartment, I heard a voice say, "Take this street". I was miles away from home and that street was not even a shorter way back to my home. I was mad, but I took that street anyway. I was tired, far from home, and wishing I had a car. Soon, I saw a man coming. The man walking towards me had one leg and here I was complaining about walking and needing a car. That same voice said to me, "Can this man drive? No, he doesn't have a car. He's walking, and he has only one leg. You have two legs. You can walk, yet you complain". So, how about this guy? What is he going to say? That was a valuable lesson I learned that day.

It's not about Oscar. It's not about you. It's about us. Our value. So, what am I saying here? The day that you were created the Creator looked at you and said you are perfect. Maybe you have been created with one eye. Maybe you have been created with one arm. Maybe you were created as a little person. When I see a person born with Down Syndrome, I pause, "Perfect? It doesn't make sense! This person could not have been created perfect!" That's because I see them with

67

natural eyes. We look at people with our natural eyes. We see that they are missing an arm or a leg or that they are blind. That's how we see them and assign them their value. This is what we're doing to these people. But, what is their real value?

I was moved by the story of an evangelist who has no legs. When he was sharing his testimony on the Internet, I couldn't even watch him or listen to him because I was hurting for this person in my soul. This was the value that I was trying to give to this person. I am not God. I was seeing a man with no legs, but his Creator doesn't see him that way. Although I have no permission to use his name or his testimony, I want to share how he has changed my life. He spoke about how much he suffered without legs. What broke my heart was when he shared how the doctor first gave the news to his parents. When he was born, the doctor said, "Your son is missing one arm! "Wait, he's missing the other one!" Soon thereafter, he told them that their son had no legs! That was a shock to his parents. He said he had thought about committing suicide a few times for this reason. However, he said that every time he thought about killing himself, he would think about his mother. He didn't want to leave his mother believing that his suicide was her fault. He knew that his mother would feel guilty because she gave birth to him and this was the way he came out.

When this man had an encounter with his Creator, it changed the way he saw himself. He didn't see himself without arms and legs, but that he was created perfect. Today, this same person is married to a beautiful wife. So, tell me, how can a beautiful woman be attracted to this man with no legs? She sees him with spiritual eyes and with all his value!

So, get up, stop crying, and stop beating up on yourself. Your situation may kill you from the inside, but I want you to stand up. Don't look at the reality, but look at the truth. You don't have what the world thinks you should have, but on the inside, you have what the Creator has given you the day He created you. You have all of His love in you. Stand up and walk! Don't see yourself through other's eyes. See yourself through God's eyes. In His eyes, you are beautiful.

When someone finds an item that is valuable, they hide it in a secret place. You are valuable. Your personality is valuable. Your identity has a lot of value. You need to take your identity and all of your value and hide it in a secret place. Don't allow anyone to come and steal that by putting you lower than that, like saying, "You are very dark skinned, you should be lighter. You should have longer hair. You should go to a dentist." They don't like what they see. As a result, people are changing their noses and mouths because people have convinced them that, if their nose were smaller and their lips were bigger, then they would have value.

There are many things people will say to devalue you and you need to stay away from that. There are words to encourage you to move forward and there are words that will drag you down. I'll give you an example. You can be a person that has put on a lot of weight. Then, you have someone you consider to be a friend being harsh with you. "Stop eating donuts or this or that!" NO! If that person gives you words that make you feel less, then you should stop listening to the negative words. You will always have negative people around you, but you need to protect yourself and get the words that are important to you.

I have a friend who I tried to encourage on the phone for several hours. She cried on the phone and didn't see herself as having any value. She lived in fear that she would lose her boyfriend. She lived day to day with insecurity and stress. I remember telling her "Yes, it's a reality that you have put on a lot of weight. If you want to lose weight, what will motivate you? Tell me what motivates you." Sometimes we have the wrong motivation. You think, "I need this job to prove myself to others, so that they will see value in me. I need that car or that big house or to dress this way or I need a promotion." Trying to prove yourself to others is the wrong motivation.

What we need to know is this: anything that you are trying to do now, someone else has already done it and way better than we think we can do it ourselves. We say, "In life, I want to be the best at this or the best at that." People have done amazing things in the past. Don't do things to prove yourself to others. Do it because you're passionate about it and your passion will   inspire others.

The woman who feared losing her boyfriend has her value tied up in her boyfriend. The fear of losing her boyfriend has made her very insecure. If she sees him talking to other girls, then she panics. If she sees Facebook comments of other women, she panics. She was unable to focus on herself. She couldn't move forward. At the time, the boyfriend left her, she was hurt. He left her because he wanted to help her focus on herself. He didn't know how to help her focus on herself. He didn't know how to handle the situation. It's often tough on the other person who doesn't know how to handle the situation. He wanted her to be happy, but he didn't know how to make her happy. I remember later telling her to focus on herself and someone else will recognize her value because she won't want anyone to treat her less than her real value.

I started encouraging my friend to work out and this is funny. I would say, "We need to go to the gym". She would go, but I wouldn't. She started losing weight and started caring more about herself, her family, and her job. She is doing fine now. She got promoted at work. The last time I visited her, she was happy.

I thought she was doing fine.

In order to love others, we need to love ourselves. You'll get there. If you don't care about yourself and allow your heart to suffer over this person you think you love or you do love, the situation won't change, and you'll keep crying. When Jesus talked about love, He said to love others like you love yourself. Think about your heart. Whenever you do something, just stop for a minute, and ask yourself, "How's that benefitting me?" Trust me, I am not trying to tell you that you need to be selfish. No. What I am saying is simple, "Love yourself."

We do things so that people will acknowledge us. There are people who will study to be a doctor or lawyer to be seen as valuable. They know that others will acknowledge their value in such careers. Maybe you have to have a higher education before your family finds value in you. Are you doing this for your family or because you love learning? Is your value in others?

Look at actors who are killing themselves to be noticed and people give them value. Are you doing this for others to call you a champion? Or are you a champion because you are passionate? On the other hand, you see girls trying hard to impress others in the way they dress, walk and talk, and wear their makeup. I am not against makeup. I bless God for seeing beautiful girls around! That is a good thing, but do you want to be pretty for yourself or do you want others to notice you? I have seen others with so much makeup that they look like zombies, when they are beautiful without the makeup. I am not attacking these things.

What is your motivation? It is not based on our eyes. I had a beautiful girlfriend and I wanted my friends to see her value because she was beautiful. I wanted my friends to approve of her and acknowledge her beauty. If they said my girlfriend was ugly, it was because they didn't see her value. What we don't know here is that the beauty that you see is not the beauty that they see. You see the beauty in her heart and that beauty influences your physical eyes. So, to you, that person becomes more beautiful to you on the outside.

That's why you hear people say, "My mother is the most beautiful person on the earth!" No offense, but I see her and think she's old and wrinkled

74

and she has marks on her face. Are you serious?" And you compare her to someone in Hollywood. You have people trying to compare their mother to a "Miss World" superstar or top model and they think she is the most beautiful person on Earth! What you don't know is that this person sees his mother's heart. So yes, I agree. She is the most beautiful person on earth. Why do I agree? It doesn't matter what you think. My mother is the most beautiful woman on earth.

I have broken up with girls just because my friends said they were ugly. The same may go for a man who is engaged and wants people to acknowledge that his fiancée is beautiful. If they comment on her dark skin, then he may say, "Maybe I should go to find someone with lighter skin. I need to go to an island and find someone who is as beautiful as an actress." I joke, but this is the reality because many people fall into that trap.

Girls, you need to understand that the way you present yourself matters. You can't sell a diamond in a ghetto. You are that special plate. Don't let anyone tell you are not worth more than a diamond and a special plate. The special plate rules exist so that people respect the special plates and don't allow just anyone to touch them. Ladies, don't let anyone convince you that you are not beautiful. I can understand that you can gain and lose weight. Don't allow people to treat you badly because they define your worth by what they see. Don't let people tell you that you are worth more if you lose weight.

Let's say that I am an artist and I create my masterpiece with blood, sweat, and hard work. I don't let anyone come to buy the art for a dollar. Leonardo Da Vinci's work is valued today at millions of dollars. The Mona Lisa is assessed at several million dollars. I couldn't go to the Louvre and offer ten dollars for the Mona Lisa. Get out of here! Everyone knows what it is worth. Don't let anyone come and take your identity away. People have told you are nothing and that you are not pretty, and you have bought into it.

I know a lot of girls beat themselves up and cry into the mirror, wishing that they were skinnier or saying that they need to gain weight and then they would feel better. Don't believe what people say—that you would be more beautiful if you had lighter or darker skin, or if you had more or less hair. These people's opinions of your beauty are not right. Your value is in your Creator. He said you are beautiful and valuable. Stay right there. I am not saying it's not right for you to lose or gain weight or to change your hair; however, your real identity is in who the Creator says you are.

I have talked to so many girls who have lost their identity to be the person that the spouse or friend wants them to be. So, if you gain weight, your friends start pressuring you to lose weight. Just look at yourself and find a real reason for why you are losing weight. Is it for them? Are you doing it for them? If so, then you are losing your identity. I would just encourage you to look at yourself. Focus on yourself. You will lose him anyway, if you don't look at yourself.

What is your motivation for losing weight? Perhaps, you cannot get a job because you are judged by your weight. It's hard for you to get a job when you are judged. You can fight for your identity. Just do it for you. Identity is not based on your physical appearance. So how can we find ourselves?

I am here talking about value, but the challenge is that you need to accept it. When they come and remind you of how valuable you are, you

77

will argue and not believe them. Why don't you want to believe the truth? That means that you agree with all these people who call you ugly, say that you are worth nothing, and that you will never accomplish anything in your life! People will come and put you down. People come and devalue you.

You have these two voices—one saying that you are valuable, and one saying you are nothing. Take time and do this as an assignment. Say these two sentences aloud. You must choose between the two. "I have so much value!" I want you to do it with all your energy, just scream and shout, "I am valuable!" Or, take the other one and with all your power and with all the energy you have, shout "I am nothing! I have no value!" What feels right? What feels good? Now, you tell me, what is the truth?

CHAPTER 5 YOU HAVE A FATHER

What we need to realize is that we are not here by accident. Maybe you grew up never knowing your father. Maybe you were adopted. Your coming to earth is not an accident. We all come in different ways. For some, it's very brutal. Maybe it's by rape and other unthinkable ways. All that matters is that you're here.

Some wonder why their mother abandoned them in the hospital. Others why their father raped their mother or why their mom got drunk and got pregnant. You can ask so many questions, and the more you ask questions, the more your heart burns and it hurts.

My assistant Robin would say the same thing: "Why was I abandoned in that hospital?" As she grew older, she wanted to find her biological mother. The more she searched without finding her biological parents, the more it hurt her. Things would have been easier had her adopted mother lied to her and not told her the truth about her real parents, but instead, she was told about her real identity. Knowing the truth about her real identity hurt. Her biological mother named her when she was born, but left her, and then she was given a new name. Thinking about all of this was painful, but who was her real mother?

Her situation made me think about the time I lost my biological mother in Africa. After it happened, I went to my friend's house for his birthday party. I couldn't stand it and I was sad and breaking into tears. My friend's mother pulled me aside and said, "Oscar, here in Africa, you don't just have one mother. All these women you see out there, they are your mothers. I'm your mother." She may not have realized it, but her words gave me strength and encouraged me, because I was hopeless and discouraged.

I had plans for what I would do with my mother and how I would bless her. My friend's mother had no idea how much her words touched and encouraged me. I used those words. I believed her. Any mother out there that I would see, I would take advantage of it. I would build a relationship with all my friends' mothers and be like a son to them. But, there was only so much each could give, even though I wanted more. I love this verse in the Bible that says, "The heart of a man plans his way, but the Lord establishes his steps" (Proverbs 16:9; ESV). That has been my story and maybe it's yours too. God has plans for you, too, that can hurt now, but will bless you later.

Someone once told me a story of a stone that didn't have value. That stone was among different, good stones that were shiny and pretty. At the time I heard this story, I was going through a lot and I was hurt. That story ministered to me. The stone didn't have value until someone came along and picked it up and wanted to increase the value of the stone. The worker who picked up the stone used a hammer to hit the stone to remove the dirt. He would even put it in a burning hot fire. He would hit it with different things and cut it with all kinds of tools.

While this man was working on the stone, the stone said, "You are killing me! You're hitting me. You don't love me. You're treating me badly." But, the stone didn't understand what was going on and it didn't understand the purpose of what this man was doing to him. It hurt! Later, when this man was done working, he put the stone back with the other stones. The other stones were like, "Wow! Is that you?" They couldn't believe it. After all the work on that stone, he became pretty and shiny, too. That stone couldn't believe it, so the other stones put a mirror in front of him and said, "Look at yourself! You are so shiny!" That's what God does for us. He works with us to increase our value and it hurts sometimes. We don't always understand why He is hurting us. The process hurts. Sometime later, when others see the transformation, they are amazed. Only the person who worked on the stone knew what was going on. Then, the stone knows how valuable it is and he cannot lose that value because he knows how tough it was to get that value.

Back to Robin's story—she told me that, at the age of 8, God told her that she would be a missionary to Africa. She had her own ideas about that message. She tried many times and many ways to get to Africa, but it never worked out because God knew what He planned, even though she believed she knew what she had to do to get there. What we need to realize is that we can't help God. Years later, she visited a Congolese church in the US. When she stepped into the door of the church, she heard God tell her Africa is here. When I heard her story, it moved me, and I never stopped telling her much how much of a blessing she has been to the Congolese people here.

At this time, she is still searching for her father. As I said earlier, she was abandoned in a hospital, where she stayed until someone came and got her. Who are her real parents: the ones who gave her birth or the ones who adopted her? The more she searched for her biological mother and father, the more she wasn't able to accept the parents that God gave her. Sometimes you can have a blessing around you and not realize how big of a blessing it is.

I think back to how I was so in love with my father. When my mom passed away, I became very attached to him. When he got sick, I prayed to God to take me and leave him here. I used to have that kind of prayer. I prayed, "God, you know what? Take me. I want him to stay". That's how much I loved that man. The devil had told me so many times, "You'll never use the word Mother anymore. You'll never have a father anymore. It's over for you." The devil was mocking me, but I knew that only God has the last word on someone's life. So, I went back and told God, "This is not what you promised me. You promised me that I would have a father and mother who love me and that I would enjoy time with them." That is what I had faith in. I believed that, but after both my mother and father were gone, I thought it was finished. It wasn't! God had a plan!

One day, I was flying to Colorado to help my cousin who was struggling during that time. She had broken up with her boyfriend, was going through a lot, and she needed support. I didn't have much money. I only had enough money to buy a ticket. I went to get her and drive back with her from Colorado to Texas. On the plane, I was sitting next to a nice lady. The fun part of this story is that I learned later that she got the last seat on that flight.

Even though I didn't know who she was, my heart was burning to talk to her, but I didn't know how to talk to her. She liked to talk and opened the conversation. We started talking and I remembered asking her if she had dogs or cats and if she had a child. She said she never had children. I started encouraging her and God began to speak through me. I said, "When we go before God, we need to go before Him and cry out like little children." I kept encouraging her throughout the flight. I didn't know who she was and she didn't know who I was, but God had a plan-- a perfect plan.

This nice lady on the plane had told me that she had been in Berlin, Germany a few months before. She went there to meet and encourage her friend and her friend's family who were missionaries there. One day, she was playing with her friend's young children. The game she was playing with them was pretending to be spies. They had to have new spy names. One of the boys, whose name was Ben, chose "Oscar" as his name and he made a drawing and named it "Oscar." Later on, as she was sorting through her things and packing for Colorado, she saw that Ben had put the "Oscar" picture in her bag. When she saw the name, it was like time stopped for a second. So, on the plane, when I told her that my name was Oscar, she understood the meaning of the picture!

So, here I was sitting next to her! I told her that I was trying to find a home church in Texas. We agreed that, when we got back to Texas, I would visit her church, which was a Baptist church. She said,

"I'll give you my number and when you get back to Texas, you call me and I will invite you to my home church". We said good-bye upon landing and went our separate ways. When I bumped into her again, we spoke for just a few seconds more and hugged each other. I knew that God had introduced me to a special lady! And so, I went on with my life. Now, I wanted a father, but I didn't have one.

One day, as I was talking to God, I became angry and said that following Him had cost me everything: my mother, my father, and my friends. I spewed a lot of angry words and told God that I was sorry and that I didn't mean it. I was being honest about my feelings. I wanted to be real with God. If you have never gotten mad at God, then you have never experienced Him in a close intimate relationship. Sometime later, after I had met up with the nice lady from the plane and had gone to church with her and her husband, I was angry with God again.

I was supposed to meet this nice couple the next day. We were at a restaurant and we were talking. The nice lady from the plane said, "We were talking, and we believe that God wants us to help you

86

with school." Then, they started talking to each other about me! They had no idea what that meant to me! They were saying, "We have to do this for him and we have to do that for him!" Wow, I heard no words coming out of their mouths, because for me, time stood still! I was speechless! This is how I pictured parents discussing what's best for their child.

So, there I was, needing a mother badly and that nice lady on the plane was needing a son just as much. She had cried out many times and God gave her a child in an unexpected way. God did it in His own way. That's how He plans things and we have to trust Him. That's the power of adoption. Her husband said that The Lord gave her a "bouncing baby"! That lady on the plane, whose name is Melissa, and her husband, whose name is Tom, became my parents. They always tell me that I am such a blessing. I share everything with my parents.

Again, that's why I love this verse Proverbs 16:9 ESV in the Bible that says: "The heart of man plans his way, but the Lord establishes his steps." God has expressed His love through my mother and father. They are not just parents to me. I have no words to describe them. They are amazing! God knows how much I love her and that she loves me and how much I love my dad and I know how much he's done for me and loves me. I know how much my Dad loves me. He doesn't have to tell me that. I feel the love of God through my mother and father. My mother always has the perfect words to say. When I ask her to pray for me, I tell her that God always answers her prayers. I can break down and cry with her. I can laugh with her and I know that she will not judge me. I cannot express how much they have blessed me.

We get angry with God because we don't understand His plans. So, while I was angry with God, and I wanted to write the story of my life. I wanted to be the author. That's why I was fascinated by Moses' story in Exodus. He wanted to write his own story and God almost killed him because of it. God is the author of life.

I always wanted to be in control of my own life. I had to surrender to God and allow Him to do things for me as a Father. He gave me parents who are examples of true love, yet their love for me is just a shadow of the Father's love for me. God showed me the power of adoption. I have learned the power of adoption. God grew my affection for Him. That's why I always say that He is a good Father. He proved to me that I could trust Him.

Recently, I interviewed my friend Deanna, who as a child grew up in a home with no father. Her sister and brother, twins, were just a little over a year younger. Her mother was absent, in that she worked twelve-fourteen hours a day. She and her siblings raised themselves. Deanna learned to be more independent. She learned not to count on anyone and felt that she couldn't. She had to be independent and to find her own way. She made her own arrangements and made her own decisions.

Growing up, Deanna did not trust relationships. She said that could be a barrier to relationships—being raised and being on her own with just her brother and sister. When asked what the struggle like, Deanna said that it was unusual to not have one's father at home. She was in grade school in the sixties and graduated high school in the seventies. For her, it was an embarrassment and not anything that she would talk about or want people to know. It was tough for her. Deanna and her siblings didn't have a loving or nurturing household. She was not in an environment where she was hugged and told that she was loved because there was no parent in the home most of the time.

When asked about her father, Deanna said that her mother had never married and that she was twenty-one when she contacted her aunt and asked about him. She went through the phone book for information, called around, found him, and met him. That proved to be a disappointment for Deanna, too! Although they met a couple of times, she found out that he had another family and had no interest in keeping a relationship with her. That door shut for her and it was discouraging.

Deanna tried to find herself by finding her father. She thought that, by finding her father, she'd found that missing part of her and the puzzle would finally make sense. She said she was hurt because she did have a glimmer of hope, only to discover that her father had no interest in keeping that connection. Over the years, she'd had some contact with her father's current family, with her half-brothers and half-sister. Yet, with them, she had no close family connection. These setbacks made it harder for Deanna to develop relationships and connections with others. It was a barrier that she had to be aware of, work on, and to understand that was still a need for her.

Deanna said that she and her siblings were there for each other as in a typical brother-sister relationship, but they were not close, nor did they do a lot of stuff together. They had each other in the house, but they didn't have a close relationship where they hugged each other and said they loved each other.

Deanna said she must have prepared herself for the discouragement with her father because she did not have that hope or feeling of closeness with him. As far as her relationship with her mother, Deanna said that they never talked about anything. She knew that her mother was closed off and private and that she had to find out information for herself. Deanna never directly asked her mother questions about her father or anything important. Even to this day, they only talk about surface topics, but nothing very deep because they don't have that type of relationship.

When asked about wanting to receive love from her siblings, Deanna said that she did, but that she had grown used to not receiving love from her family. So, after she had children and loved them so much, Deanna started thinking about how she wanted to raise them in church. When they were small, she made the commitment to Christ. Motherhood changed her and the way she looked at things. She still struggles with the effect of not growing up with close relationships, not having loving parents or involved parents, and having obstacles to overcome. Because she grew up without the love she wanted, Deanna hugged her kids and often told them that she loved them, and she still does today. Deanna said that she thought that motherhood and her commitment to Christ were the starts of her finding herself.

What Deanna learned over the years was to hold on to her faith—the mustard seed faith—through the difficulties, valleys, and doubts that life brings. When asked if not having her father affected her connection with Christ as her spiritual Father, Deanna said that it did and believes that's true for people who have never experienced an earthly father's love. They feel unworthy to   accept Christ's love.

As a child, Deanna "really kind of dabbled" in church. Her mother really didn't go to church, and even though she was sometimes invited to church and youth group, Deanna didn't attend regularly. She said that those times planted some seeds and she often thought about Christ. So, when she had children and experienced that love for them, Deanna said that it helped her to be better able to accept Christ's love. Deanna still carries some anger toward her father and mother, but she understands their lives. They were young and now that she is older, Deanna can put herself in their shoes.

When asked how she identifies herself, Deanna said that she is a mother, a wife, a child of God, and a good employee who tries to be what everybody wants her to be. She said she is more of a pleaser, but she wants to be who she is and who God made her to be. Deanna said that she knows there are good people who don't know Christ and there are some people who are troubled.

Deanna believes that any good thing she does is in the name of Christ. It's because of His promptings –not that she hears an audible voice—that she does good works. She understands that others do good works and she cannot question their motives. They may not be believers, but do good works, whether it's for themselves or for other reasons.

When asked about the possibility of losing one's identity, Deanna said that she believes that we can struggle to the point where we are confused about our identity. She thinks that we can feel weak in those areas, like for example, when she moved out of state and knew no one, she felt weak as a mother. That's when Deanna felt like she lost her identity, not literally, but that she lost who she said she was. Deanna still had her identity, but at that time, she was struggling to figure that out.

Since finding herself was one of the good things that happened to Deanna, I asked what she would say to those of us out there who are still looking for our identity. When Deanna was divorced after many years of marriage, she was at odds, unsettled, in turmoil. She would cry out to the Lord and read devotionals and the Bible while she was still in anguish—it was a painful process.

During that time, while listening to Christian radio, and doing what she was supposed to be doing—going to work and doing everything she knew to do—something happened. She was in her little apartment with a candle burning. Soon, it dawned on her that, in being consistent in doing all those things amid turmoil, she had finally become content and at peace for the first time in a long time. Deanna knew that this is who she was and that she was okay.

She remembered that moment in 2004 when her work week ended on a Friday night with that weekend ahead of her. Monday seemed so far away. She was wrapping Christmas presents and realized that she was at peace. She said that being a child of God was central to her identity. She is, in a word, a Christian or a believer (specifically in Christ).

I believe that we all need that guidance from a father, that voice of authority over us—the voice of discipline. At the same time, it is the voice of encouragement and support—the voice that fills you with words of love. It doesn't matter how old you are, but your soul, body, and spirit need it in so many ways. Some deny or some ignore it, but when it's a fact, it hurts. I believe that it is a need to have this.

It starts when you're honest with yourself, and I say, "I need a father". You can see your father in anyone. It is a gift from God. I myself needed a father. I was honest, looked for him, searched for him, and I found him—in God and in Tom. I found a father, but I didn't know that I was next. Somebody was out there searching for me. I will go ahead and share the words of that person who was searching for me.

It was on Christmas. He wrote in my card, "I know a lot about the best things in life because I have one of them. I have you for my Dad." Never in my life had I ever read something like this. That froze my heart and it was like all feelings hit me at the same time—I was freezing and burning. I tried to compare this feeling to being in love, but this feeling was more than that. It was strange. It was the first time I experienced that kind of love. These words came from a young boy, Cedar, an orphan looking for his father. I guess I didn't have any choice because he had adopted me to be his father. He texts me every day in the morning when he wakes up and before he goes to bed. If I don't text back, I'll get in trouble because he will call me out on it.

This is a different gift on top of what God has given me to have a father, but now He is even allowing me to experience what it means to be a father, just to show me that it is a responsibility and that He is responsible. Like I have said, He has shown me that through Tom my father. He will travel just to spend time with me. He will make time. He is a busy man, but he tries his best to make time to call me.

We talk every week and know what's going on in each other's lives. Learning that from him allows me to know how to cherish my love and relationship with God and how I must apply that same love and relationship to Cedar.

So, one thing I will tell you is to be honest with yourself. If you need a father, open your heart. Be real about your feelings. I'm pretty sure that there is a father out there who wants to adopt you. There's a father out there who loves you and wants to give you all the love that you need. And I know about the best Father—God! He knows all your needs. He has been out there waiting for you and ready to love you. I know that by reading these words, you'll be so mad at Him. It's a good thing. Just open your heart.

You can be mad at God, but be open about that and open your heart. Anger keeps us from getting there. We're angry about so many things and ask so many questions. That's what I am trying to tell you. You're trying to write your story. Let God write your story. I understand that it hasn't been easy. Maybe that's what you need—to go out there and grab and take all the love of a father that you can from those people who love you and value you. You see, you want your father to look a certain way. You want to give him an image. You have designed your own father—how he should look, talk and so on.

I had also designed my own father, but I had to learn to trust God. I had to trust God and say, "Whatever You have". That's what I am telling you. Read this book with an open mind. I was mad. It took me a while to say, "I surrender.' I was mad, but had to surrender and say, "Do whatever you want. Your will be done." That's how I got there. That's how you'll get there. Also, it will not work if you say, "I want it right now." Open your heart and tell Him to come in. Tell Him, "I want Your love." He will welcome you.

CHAPTER 6 LOVE

One thing we need to know about love is that love is like a muscle. Thinking of love as a muscle makes me think of a past workout. A friend was watching me. During that time, I was building up my muscles, but he didn't say anything. I worked out day after day. It wasn't easy, but I was consistent. I was very self-motivated, but my friend wouldn't say anything. He just watched me and never said anything.

Then one day, I decided to quit. My friend waited until I had lost all my muscles to say, "Wow, when you were working out, you had gained a lot of muscles, but I watched and waited for the day when you would quit and lose all your muscles before I could talk to you." I was so disappointed. Had he come to me and told me that I was doing well, he would have kept me going. Those words would have kept me going, but he waited until I was done and had quit to tell me that.

Do not wait for people to come and tell you, "Oh, you are a lovely person. You are so kind." Sometimes, people will not tell you that. They will watch you and wait for the day that you screw up, and then they will come and tell you and say, "Wow, you used to be a good person, and you did this, and you did that. But, look at what you did today. We're so disappointed. We're so disgusted. We can't believe you did this or did that". You're doing fine. Keep doing whatever you're doing. Don't wait for anyone.

You will get tired. There will be times when you feel like you just want to give up and quit loving people. There are times when you will feel like you don't want to do it anymore. There will be times when you feel like no one deserves your love. There will be times when you feel like you're being abused by people. That's the time when you want to push through. That's the time when you want to give more. It will be tough, but you must be on top of it because you are a lovely person. That's your heart.

The more you exercise love, the more it grows. Remember earlier in the book when I was talking about how I lost it. I was born in love and ready to love, but I didn't know how to love. I didn't know the meaning of love or even how to love people. Most of us think that love is an easy thing. No, it's the hardest thing you will ever imagine, but it is part of our identity. It is hard, but one thing that I have come to discover about love is that you give it. You give it. I mean it is easier when you give it.

Love is made to be given. If you do otherwise, that's when it hurts. You have love because someone gave it to you. It was made to be given from the very beginning. You have received love. When you were a child, you were given love. It helped you to become stronger and more confident as you were growing up. At some point, when you realize that you have love to give and you don't give it to someone else, then that is when the conflict comes. It was made to be given.

When you don't give love and when you keep it to yourself, you'll end up in crisis. Just imagine mothers. I don't know if it is the reality here in the United States, but in Africa, sometimes it is hard for mothers to love, but they give it away. They give it. I believe that it is just a reality for every mother in the world.

Children can be a challenge. You don't really know if they love you back yet when they are little, but you love them whether they respond or don't respond. You love them. So, it's easy that way—to give love to a child is easy. When they start growing up, then you may think, "I have given them so much love. Now, I want something in return." That's when the conflict comes.

A mother has expectations, and when her child grows up, she says, "I have invested so much in my child. I wish she would love me back!" That causes the crisis. Some mothers can handle it and some mothers cannot handle it. A lot of mothers enter a big crisis, because they realize how much they did for their children when they were kids. Recently, I was talking to my friend's mother. She had a conflict because her son doesn't want her, his sisters, or any other family members to be a part of his life.

What his mother told me that really captured my attention were her words: "Oscar, if only God can take him back to see how he was born and how he grew up and all the events that he doesn't remember or think of...if only God could show him how his childhood was...what I did..." As she spoke, I was able to read the pain of that mother. She said, "That same child I was there for and I did a lot for him and now he's gone. It almost killed me." When things happened that way, it was her crisis because she thought about how much she did and how much she invested in this friend of mine—and now he's gone. He doesn't want to have anything to do with her. That was her crying out for love.

Sometimes we have a misconception of love. We see it as a bank account: the more we put in, the more we will be able to take out. Or, we see it more as a tax return: the more taxes are taken out, the bigger the return. It doesn't work that way. You can give a lot of love and get back a little. Or, you can give a lot and get nothing in return. One of the things to avoid when it comes to love is to expect something in return. Expecting something in return opens the door to crisis because the minute you don't get it back, you get upset.

What kills us is the expectation. I pay out a lot in taxes during the year, but I may not get much of a tax return. The more taxes they take out, the bigger my return...or so I thought. There have been times when the government took out a lot of taxes during the year and I got less. I was upset. It's the same thing with love. When you're expecting a lot and you get less, it hurts you.

But when you give it out and you don't expect or have high expectations, sometimes you get even more. And even if it's a little, you still feel good because your expectation wasn't high. Keep giving it away because, sometimes, you may get more than you expected.

As I said in an earlier chapter, it was easier for me to love when I was a child because I didn't have a question whether people loved me or not. I was a giver. But as I grew older, this question came up, "I love people, but does anyone love me in return?" I know you, my reader, might want to argue with me on this, but let's keep going. Maybe later you will agree with me that love is made to be given.

Mothers, the way God made them, will respond. When you give them love, they will give it back, but now I have a mother who's gone. I am not saying that this is the reality with every mother. Sometimes they just can't give love because they themselves are in some sort of crisis. In general, mothers give back whatever you give them, but then, my mother wasn't here anymore, so I was trying to exchange love, give it and get it back, but it didn't work with my father, siblings, girlfriend or my friends. It didn't work out. Why? It was because I wanted something in return. I wanted to be loved too. The reality is that love is a gift—it's something that you give away. The minute that you want it back, it stops working.

Let's talk more about love being a muscle. It is a reality of God Himself. Just read the Bible. In Genesis 6, God repented that He had created human beings, but He never gave up on them. He did repent, but later, He was still there. He did repent—or we would not have had Jesus Christ. Jesus came because God never gave up on man. That love grew, but there were challenges.

One of the challenges is in the prophecy of Isaiah Chapter 5. God told His children, "I have given you everything that you could possibly imagine, but in return, look at what you're doing!" God was even trying to find a witness between Him and man. So, if I am arguing with a child and I think I am right and the child is wrong, then I want to go and get a third party. You're speechless when the child argues with you and you want a witness to prove that you are right. God wanted to have a witness and, even if that were possible, the situation was unbelievable—that of trying to find a witness between Him and man. It's like an adult trying to find a witness between herself and the child. God is saying, "Who is going to understand me? Will somebody just understand me?"

Does God really have to argue with us? No, but these words from the prophet Isaiah are to help us to understand God's love for us. God says, "No one can give back to Me what I have given." All of this is to make us understand how much He loves us. Let me explain.

In order for a man to get married in Congo, he has to get ready. Your future wife's family will have to give you a list of gifts for the father and mother and the dowry for the bride. The man will save money, start getting organized, buy a house, and then prepare the house to be ready for his wife. Before he can prepare the house, he has to meet the parents and pay the dowry. Different cultures have different dowries. Maybe you have to buy suits and goats for the father and shoes for the mother. Then, once that is done, the wife comes home. She will feel loved when she comes home.

In Genesis 1, God prepared the earth, made a garden and the animals, and then created man last. When a Congolese man argues with his wife, he will say, "I have done this and this and worked hard for you, and this is what I deserve?" If the wife cheats on her husband, then the man is upset because he invested so much money and time, only to be repaid this way.

What do we do in this case? Do we give up on this person because we are hurt? God doesn't give up on us. He is a giver. In Matthew 19:1-12, the Pharisees asked Jesus about love and marriage and what to do with a wife who cheats. The passage says: "Now when Jesus had finished these sayings, he went away from Galilee and entered the region of Judea beyond the Jordan. And large crowds followed him, and he healed them there. And Pharisees came up to him and tested him by asking, "Is it lawful to divorce one's wife for any cause?" He answered, "Have you not read that he who created them from the beginning made them male and female, and said, 'Therefore a man shall leave his father and his mother and hold fast to his wife, and the two shall become one flesh'? 6 So they are no longer two but one flesh. What therefore God has joined together, let not man separate." They said to him, "Why then did Moses command one to give a certificate of divorce and to send her away?" He said to them, "Because of your hardness of heart Moses allowed you to divorce your wives, but from the beginning, it was not so. And I say to you: whoever divorces his wife, except for sexual immorality, and marries another, commits adultery." The disciples said to him, "If such is the case of a man with his wife, it is better not to marry." But he said to them, "Not everyone can receive this saying, but only those to whom it is given. For there are eunuchs who have been so from birth, and there are eunuchs who have been made eunuchs by men, and there are eunuchs who have made themselves eunuchs for the sake of the kingdom of heaven. Let the one who is able to receive this receive it."

Love was meant to be forever. Don't give up on that person. That is Christ's personality. It's not easy. That's why I say love is the hardest thing ever. It wasn't easy for Christ to go to the Cross—it was hard for Him. Real love has to face challenges, will show your character, and has to be tested. The test of the love of God was the Cross—go on and heal the pain and prove that you are a lover. Jesus's love was judged. People judged and questioned it and, but He went until the end—to the Cross. He was judged and condemned, but His love overcame the condemnation because that love didn't plead guilty.

We all have to be innocent in the judgments placed on us and on the judgments we place on others. It can be family, a friend, a job, or people who challenge and question your love. Some will even doubt that you are a lover. In the end, you must prove that you are a lovely person. Was it easy? No! We all have a cross and we try to avoid it. I understand you. I don't want my cross, but love has a cost. We all have that moment like in Isaiah 5, but the most beautiful moment of love is when we say, "I am going to take this cup."

But that was God's love growing and given to man. Love is something that man wants, and man doesn't even understand the deal or know the meaning of love. It is a like a balloon with a hole in it. It doesn't matter how much air you put in, it's going to leak out. That's what God wants to do, to fix us so that we can receive His love. He wants to help the person be ready to receive love.

I learned about love when I stopped being selfish. The more I love others, the more I feel alive. What God was trying to give them—that love was so much. As human beings, we love so much, but imagine God's love? Can you imagine the love from the One Who created love? We think that we love so much, but we're still not at the top. I think here on earth we have a glimpse of that love, what it feels like. Here love is not perfect.

1 Cor 13:4-13 ESV says: "Love is patient and kind; love does not envy or boast; it is not arrogant or rude. It does not insist on its own way; it is not irritable or resentful; it does not rejoice at wrongdoing, but rejoices with the truth. Love bears all things, believes all things, hopes all things, endures all things. Love never ends. As for prophecies, they will pass away; as for tongues, they will cease; as for knowledge, it will pass away. For we know in part and we prophesy in part, but when the perfect comes, the partial will pass away. When I was a child, I spoke like a child, I thought like a child, I reasoned like a child. When I became a man, I gave up childish ways. For now, we see in a mirror dimly, but then face to face. Now I know in

part; then I shall know fully, even as I have been fully known. So now faith, hope, and love abide, these three; but the greatest of these is love."

That is what perfect love is. Here on earth, we have to grow that love. We will not experience perfect love until Heaven. Love sometimes is judged, but we don't need to plead guilty. Your love will lead you to the cross. Others will judge you and condemn you. It has to be judged, but it is real. Sometimes we will feel that love is dead, but it's not. Your love is not dead. It is still there. Your love will overcome.

Suppose someone cheated on you, but you didn't give up—you went on the cross and it looked as though your love was dead. God will come with His power and revive your love. There is a power that will come and raise it from the grave. Sometimes people will test and question your love. People will try to bring out the worst part of you and create a false testimony of you. People condemned Christ and He was executed, but His love rose from the dead. Maybe you feel like you're at the place where your love is dead. No! The power of Living Love will come to you and raise your love from the dead. You can experience passion with others. I'm not saying it's easy.

When we were children we acted like children. As you become mature, you gain wisdom and your love grows, too. I can relate to that because, when I was trying to give the love that I had for my mother to my girlfriend or friend and they were afraid, they asked: "Man, what are you doing?" That was a lot. That is the same deal with God. He was trying to give it to us and we weren't ready to get it. We don't even get it or understand it, but He was giving it to us. When you come to John 3:16, the Bible says, "God so loved the world, that He gave His Only Son…" He gave. Love is a gift and, most of the time, we think that you give it to people who "deserve" it—not true. Love is even for those who don't deserve it. That's how they get transformed.

Most of the time, love is for people who don't deserve it, and when they get it, it transforms their lives. They didn't deserve it. No one deserves God's love, but He gave us that love. The times when I've gotten it and thought, "Oh! So that's why!" It took me time to understand that. Once I got it, I realized that love is to be given. Love is not what you get, but what you give to people.

It becomes a challenge because, when you give and nobody wants it and no one is ready to receive it, that's when it hurts a lot. I know you might be out there trying to love someone who doesn't want it, but if you want it, you have to give it!

I believe that's love. It's hard even now and will never get easier, but I believe that, the more I exercise it, the more my love becomes stronger. Like I said, it's like a muscle. Don't go practice on people who deserve it--that's too easy. You practice on a person who does not deserve it—the person who raped you, stole from you, or killed your family member. Those are the people you go practice this love with. The more you practice, the greater your love becomes, but it's not a painless process.

It is not easy, but what we need to understand is that love is part of our identity. It's part of you and, once you lose it, you get lost. You were born to love. It's part of you. You are a lovely person. The conflict starts when people start responding badly. I understand that you may have a lot of bad experiences with people whom you tried to love, and they took advantage of you and your good heart, but the thing is that you need to love people. Loving someone means that you have to give them whatever they want. No! What you're feeling about that person who is trying to take advantage of your money—you have to love him. You don't just give him money. You love him, which doesn't mean buying him stuff. He needs prayer. Pray for this person to find his way.

Learn to love this person in a different way. We want people to change, but we don't love them. Love is what rose Lazarus from the grave. Love causes miracles to happen. Why is our world falling apart? We want love, but we are not loving others. In any relationship, we come with the mindset about what we will get from the person. Jesus did things for people that He asked them to keep secret between them. That's love. If you want to see someone's life transformed, love them.

Most of the people who are messed up think they don't deserve love. We make it worse when we judge them. You hurt them even more and you kill them. You can argue with me, but you have never experienced what I have. Everyone has experienced bad things, but if you want to see transformation, then love that person. Love that person!

I have seen very violent people become soft through the power of love. The power of love will transform a whole community. Martin Luther King. Jr. loved people. It was about people. How do all of these great people accomplish remarkable things? Most of the people who have moved the world and marked time did so with love. Love builds. Love calls things into existence that didn't exist. That's what love does.

Can you learn to love? Yes. Do people who first meet each other really love each other? No. When you see this person for the first time, have butterflies in your stomach, and you feel burning inside, it's nice, but it is not loving someone. It's the same with any relationship.

You have a child who frustrates you and you want to kill her, but that is only a feeling. You really love her. I know that this is a silly example, but I just want to illustrate what real love is. It doesn't happen overnight. It takes time. Feelings change over time. Love grows over time and it becomes a strong muscle. A baby eats and doesn't make decisions, so it's easy for a parent to love her. Then she grows up and it becomes more complicated and difficult. Love is put to a test. Love is loving your child even when your child does the opposite of what you expect. Even God put His love to the test. Genesis chapter 6 is one of my favorite passages: Genesis 6:5-6 ESV says, "God was sorry that He had made man on earth. And it grieved Him in His heart." A lot of people are shocked at how I can love this passage, but it is because I understand what is going on. God is stretching out His muscles. This is extraordinary! This is true love. It's like seeing a lion in action. I like the version that said God "repented," but we know He never gave up on man. Hebrews chapter 1 tells us how God has shown us His love in many ways and many times.

Fear can be a barrier because love is a test. Fear is part of that test and stops us from experiencing the true meaning of love. It's sometimes because of what we have experienced in the past. We have presented our love and people took advantage of it and people have used us. So, because of our past experiences, we don't want to give any more love. You might say, "Okay, I will be in a relationship, but I'm not going to love. I'm not going to give my heart. I'm just going to give my brain. I will get married, but I am never going to love my husband (or my wife). This whole experience will be a brain experience." Relationships are not just brain experiences.

Mostly, the heart experiences the heart. I'm not saying that you don't have to use your brain, but it's the heart that makes that experience. A relationship without the heart is not a relationship—it's more like a business. It's a business transaction: "I am going there to get that, and if I'm not in, then I'm out."

Love is a gift, but no one wants to give it away. But if you don't give it away, then it's hard to receive it. When you give it to someone, then you start transforming that person and that person starts to give it back. Here is the fun part. You don't even expect it, but you get it. Most of us we are not givers, we are receivers. Most of us don't want to give, but we want to receive.

Love needs to be tested. If it's always about us, then that is the wrong perspective. Like I said, love is a gift. The more you love that person, the more that person will be transformed, and that person will love you back. It's like pouring water into a glass. The more you pour into the glass, the more it fills. Eventually, it overflows, and it touches you and others. It's the same with love. A lack of love causes people to become violent and then comes crisis.

One day, I saw a video on the Internet about a young man. Some people came and killed his mother and father. Then, he went and killed the people who killed his parents. Soon, he began stealing from and killing people in South Africa. This man needed love. His parents were gone and he lost his resources and foundation. If someone would love him, then I believe that he would find himself. He needs love, and then he would be transformed. No one wants to give love. We want people to appreciate us, but we aren't ready to love.

I was also moved by a story of a lady in Washington, DC. One day, her husband woke up, left the house, and never returned. For five years, the wife waited, prayed, asked, and hoped that he will return. She prayed the same prayer for five years. I have never prayed for the same thing for more than two years. She really loved him and love will lead you to pray the right way. She still loved even though he left her. She had a right to leave him, but she didn't. Love is hard. It hurts. If you haven't experienced hurt, then you haven't experienced love.

I know of couples who fight and think they want to kill each other almost every day. People are driven to this point. I am not married, but I have heard stories and know it isn't easy. What keeps couples together for so long? It is love. The time that you wanted to leave and you walked out of the house—it was love that pulled you back. Love is not for sale. It is a gift that you give with a pure heart. Once you give love away, it's a gift. It's not yours to take back.

I know you might be out there trying to love someone who doesn't want it, but you give it away anyway. It feels like you have this box that you don't want, so you go out and throw it in the trash. "I don't want it. Do you want it? You can have it." You could tell people that it's a box of shoes to donate or a box of money. If you leave the box of donated shoes on a doorstep and try to come back for it, it's going to be gone. If you see someone wearing your shoes, you can't go up to them and take them back. It's the same with love: it's the responsibility of the other person. Sometimes you love someone, they receive that love and become transformed. Sometimes, you give love to someone and they treat you badly or take advantage of you.

Children have parents who love and nurture them. When the child grows up, he will either accept that love or he won't—that is his responsibility. Some people will not take care of the gift of love that they are given. Some will take care of it and it will flourish and others will destroy it. You might have your box of love out there and nobody will recognize it. You have to wait for the person who wants to take it. Be patient. Don't hurt yourself in the meantime. Put your box out there and be patient until the right person comes along, sees its value, and picks it up. Wait. Love is a light and only the people who step out of the darkness will accept the love. Step into the light. Don't hide your light and love. You are lovely. Let your love shine, embrace that light, and allow others to embrace it back.

CHAPTER 7 BLESSED OR CURSED

Am I blessed or cursed? That's a question so many gifted people ask themselves. There are people who are talented and nations that are rich and blessed with natural resources. So, they find themselves with a gift, but it feels like a curse because it is a gift that people take advantage of for themselves. In the process, these gifted people have an identity crisis. They want to get away from the gift, thinking that it will heal them or help them to find themselves.

What's the real problem? Is it the gift itself, or the person or the country that has the gifts, or is it people who come and exploit the gift? There are so many questions. We all wonder if power and the understanding of it is the issue or if it is more so a matter of who needs or earns it. They have a gift that they want to give and bless others with but, sometimes it costs them a lot. It costs them their identity. It costs them their lives. It's so hard.

Whether it's in the workplace, church, or in the community, people don't always realize how much it costs you to give what you have and to share your gifts. You become the center of attention. Some people won't like you and some people are jealous, even though it's not about competition. It's just you are giving your gift. They have a gift they want to give, too. It's challenging when God gives you so much. At times, you tell Him to take the gift away because now you feel cursed. And, when you don't give it, you feel like you're not alive because you know you are called to share that gift. It's even more difficult at work because your gift is used all the time and some people around you don't understand that you are simply using your gift. They will get mad and some won't like you. The same reality exists in the church. You are using your gift, but it becomes a problem.

It's just like that in the Congo. Many people have talked about what's happening there. I am not the first, but I ask you to consider this: is the Congo blessed or cursed? The Congo is a country that is blessed by God. Excluding the eastern part of the Congo, we can see how blessed the nation is. You can plant any kind of seed in your backyard and it will grow because the soil is so fertile. It's part of the Congo.

You can also find all kinds of materials in the Congo, such as "Limitless water, from the world's second-largest river, the Congo, a benign climate, and rich soil make it fertile, beneath the soil abundant deposits of copper, gold, diamonds, cobalt, uranium, coltan and oil are just some of the minerals that should make it one of the world's richest countries[2]." Water from the Congo River is a precious natural resource, yet some people don't have access to water. If you want to have good water to drink, then you must spend a lot of money on it. There are also minerals in the Congo yet to be discovered. You'd be amazed to see how blessed the Congo is, but the people there feel like they are under a curse, especially when it comes to the coltan in the eastern part of the Congo.

That land is so rich. The Congo has the second largest tropical rainforest in the world[3]. Scientists sometimes call rainforests the 'lungs' of Earth. Rainforests also help to stabilize the Earth's climate. Without them, the sun could burn the earth. We need them so that the world can protect itself against the sun or else we will get burned. It is playing a significant role, but for the people who are living in the east

[2] (www.bbcmagazine.com 9 October 2013 Dan Snow).
[3] " (www.wonderopolis.com "Wonder of the Day #667 "Why are Rainforests important? 2014–2018 © National Center for Families Learning).

part of Congo, it is a curse. We see the Congo as blessed. No! It doesn't feel like it's blessed. Wars never stop. Many of the children born and growing up in war won't make it. They die along the way. War—bombs flying all over, guns shooting all over—is life in the east part of Congo. Yet, the land is so blessed. Is it really a blessing or is it a curse?

People are dying because of the riches found in the eastern part of the Congo. Imagine the prayer of the young child who lost his mother from a bullet to her head or a bomb exploding next door. Families are falling apart with no hope for the future at all.

I remember the story of a man who told me that he saw his own mother shot in front of him. He and his family were trying to escape the eastern part of Congo. The father left first. He left his wife and children with money to pay the rebels. When she refused to pay them, the rebels shot her. He said, "I didn't know how to express my feelings. Should I cry? Should I...My heart was turned into something else." Imagine the prayers of people in that land. Imagine how many times the people of the Congo have wanted to give up on their identity so that they would have peace. Sometimes, we who are Congolese wish that we were not born in that nation.

What I see in the United States is how proud people are of the nation and its flag. In contrast, I have heard Congolese people of say, "Why don't we just sell our country? Let's just sell it, because we are tired. We can just sell our nation." Americans are proud of their nation, but some people have lost that pride in the Congo. You'll hear Congolese people say that they wish they could sell their land, country, nation because they are tired of the oppression and they feel powerless. They want to defend themselves, but they can't. Is it really a blessing or a curse? It is easy for me to talk about the Congo because I am from there, but what about different nations that have paid a price for oil or another precious natural resource?

Reading my words alone is not enough to express the horrors in the Congo. You would be shocked by what people don't know about it. People don't know about women getting raped and sodomized by soldiers' weapons. You cannot even imagine how people are being tortured. The rebels beat babies with the same large sticks and wooden bowls used to beat cassava leaves until they become like pieces of processed meat. They even chop up babies to pieces with machetes. These are horrible things you cannot imagine that people are doing to one another in the Congo.

The reason is that they were "blessed," but is it really a blessing? Our land is blessed, but at the price of much of our blood. We talk about genocide with the Holocaust, but it is also part of our story in the Congo, and it is still happening. It's the Great War of Africa—the world's bloodiest conflict since World War II--within the borders of the Congo. In this war, more than five million people have died, millions have faced starvation and disease, and several million women and girls have been raped[4]. The death toll since the Congo war began is more than the genocide of the Holocaust and both World Wars combined. Many children don't know their fathers raped their mothers…

---

[4] (Dan Snow DR Congo: Cursed by its natural wealth. 9 October 2013. Par. 1-3. Copyright © 2018 BBC. BBC News Services. www.bbc.com/news/magazine-24396390 24 April 2018.)

I always wonder what people there are thinking. Some of them don't even know. They see the war and don't understand the why. How many people feel like they want to give up? Many are tempted to commit suicide because they have a gift, but now they feel like it is a curse.

It happens in so many ways. You see, countries like the Congo are blessed with all kinds of minerals. Without the eastern part of the Congo, you wouldn't have a cell phone or computer. Even nuclear weapons that people have created to make wars come from the uranium in the eastern part of the Congo. This beautiful country with precious natural resources is supposed to be a blessing, but now it's a curse. Who makes this a curse?

Gifted people wonder if they should call it gifts, because their own gifts have cost them their lives. There are many out there. I am just using an example of a country, but maybe it's you, my reader. You have wanted to give up because you feel like you have been abused for your gift. You have so much to give, but you don't want to give it because people have taken advantage of you. People have abused you. Maybe it's your beauty that men have abused, but know that you have to fight for what was given to you! You have to fight for your gift, so that people know that you matter and that your voice matters. It doesn't matter how long you live. Some people in life care about you. What matters is the quality of the life that you have. Some people who have changed the world have died young.

You have to give all your gifts, as much as you can, but don't suffer at the hands of others from it. Your gifts were given to you to share with the world. I know there are people out there who will come and take advantage of you, but you must be out there. You might be gifted in sports, but you feel like that you don't enjoy your gifts because people come and take it. Whether you are an athlete, singer, or anyone else with a valuable gift, you feel pressured by the person who trains you or benefits from your gift. And, it's not just the trainer, but also other people who have lofty expectations for you. You give, give, and give until you feel like you have nothing left. You are tired and think, "Is this really a gift or am I cursed?"

Sometimes we think it's easier to put it on display. In the Congo, it's not that easy because there are people out there who are ready to use and take advantage of you. When you have a gift, not everyone you give it to will appreciate it. Here I am talking about the story of the Congo. Not everyone who goes to the Congo goes with a bad heart. There are people who go to the Congo to bless them and work with them. They want to do honest business with them and come to create jobs. On the other hand, there are those who come to take advantage of, kill, and exploit us for whatever it is they are after. You don't want to look at those people. Look at people who come with pure hearts who want to bless you by helping you to develop your gifts for everyone's benefit.

There are other people who, when they see you, see a million-dollar opportunity. They're like, "Oh, you're so talented" while thinking, "So, how can we use you and make money?" You become a business and don't really matter to them. They don't care whether you have second thoughts about what they're doing, about your emotions, nor about how you are doing.

Don't let things like that stop you from using your gifts. You have to have a balance. The people who genuinely enjoy and are blessed by your gifts are the people you need to look at. It's not a matter of what you get out of it or how many people enjoy what you have because a gift is made to be given. So, the less you give, the more you suffer. It's challenging when you're trying to give when they oppress you. I know it's hard, but remember that your gift was made to be given. Peace is what you will get when you give your gift. I'll give you an example.

A man who delivers mail is frustrated because the traffic is bad. If he turns around and goes home, then he will no longer have a job because he never delivered that mail. It has to go to its destination because that's his job, even if he becomes frustrated. If he goes back home, then his job is not done. He needs to go to that destination. It might be tough and you may have to find a different road to take, but if there's no other way, then fight. Fight! Don't let that traffic stop you. Be there as much as you can, but make sure you get to the place of destination and you deliver that gift.

Whether your gift is music, sports or something else, make sure you give it. That's how you will find peace.

Remember the gift that Jesus had. It wasn't easy for Him to go and deliver that gift, but He made sure that we got the gift. There was traffic. There was opposition. When there is opposition and people put pressure on you, they take what's in you. Think about a balloon. If pressure is put on it, it releases air. The same thing happened to Christ. Many people came, applied pressure, and what came out was His love for mankind. People came and said all kinds of things and questioned His motives. "Why did He do that? He should do it this way, and not in that way!" People wanted Him to give His gift in their ways. Despite all these things—whatever people said and whatever judgment they put on Him—He didn't stop giving His gift, which was to be given on the cross. That's when it hurts the most.

We all have that moment, but you have to make sure that you go to the end to give that gift. Persevere no matter how many distractions hold you up or how many people question your motives and tell you that you have nothing to give. Many people get

132

discouraged because others have told them, "Well, you're not a good singer. Give up. There's no way you'll ever play sports! Look at you!"

I love the story of a famous soccer player. When he was young, he was sick and there was no way he could play soccer. Yet, today he has made it through and is very famous because he didn't give up on giving his gift. He dealt with a lot of traffic and today, he's one of the greatest soccer players of all time. Don't think that it'll be easy for you. It's very challenging.

The stories I've told you—and the Congo has many other stories out there—are a wake-up call for you. I want you to see how many people are dying out there and didn't have a chance to use their gifts. You and I have many opportunities in front of us. Can we cry and say that things are not fair to us? How about those other guys? You have a lot of room to use your gifts, so make sure you use them.

What we also need to do is to learn how to appreciate other people's gifts. When we don't, we are no different than an oppressor, someone who's jealous, or a killer. We don't want to be in that position.

We want to appreciate other people's gifts. If you don't know how to do it, that's because it is not your gift, so don't even fight for it. See that gift in someone else, bless God for it, and bless that person to be able to use his gift. Give him enough room to use his gift and push him to use it! That's how it has to be. I have learned to love and appreciate other people's dreams. We all need to learn to do that. That's how it's supposed to be.

We don't have the same gifts. We have different gifts and talents. What is not yours is not yours. Allow other people to have theirs. As I said earlier, it is not a competition. It doesn't matter whether you think yours is more or yours is less—enjoy what you have!

CHAPTER 8 HUMAN IDENTITY

What happened to us? That is the question that most of us who are concerned ask ourselves. We wonder what has happened to us as human beings, where did we go wrong, and how did we lose it. We used to be one. We used to love one another. We were going in the same direction, but what happened? We were called to be one people. We were called to be one race, yet we're divided. A lot of people are concerned, but most don't have the courage to speak out. What has happened? I don't want to talk about what's happening now, but let's go back and see what happened in history.

What were we doing in the first place? We were fighting each other. We were killing each other because of the fear of anybody who looks different from you. There's a lot of confusion among us. Perhaps, I should say you'll see that every race is prideful, saying that we are superior to someone else because of the way we look. One example of conflict among nations is when Rwanda and Uganda became allies with Laurent Kabila to bring down Zaire dictator Mobutu Sese-

Seko, but soon after, these two countries were against each other.

Another example is what happened between two ethnic groups within Rwanda—the Tutsis and the Hutus—who are the same people! "Between April and July 1994, hundreds of thousands of Rwandans were murdered in the most rapid genocide ever recorded. The killers used simple tools – machetes, clubs and other blunt objects, or herded people into buildings and set them aflame with kerosene. Most of the victims were of minority Tutsi ethnicity; most of the killers belonged to the majority Hutus[5]". These ethnic groups, from the same country, these brothers, slaughtered each other. From the largest category of people down to the smallest and most personal category—race to country to ethnicity to villages to families and finally to brothers and sisters—there was fighting, killing, conflict, and war. You'll see one nation trying to eliminate the other nation to gain power. Why are these two tribes—the Tutsis and the Hutus—in conflict? Each wants to be in power. You see the same thing in the Congo.

[5]https://www.theguardian.com/news/2017/sep/12/americas-secret-role-in-the-rwandan-genocide "America's secret role in the Rwandan genocide" 12 September 2017. Par. 1

The neighboring countries both say, "Let's kill as many Congolese as we can so that we can be in power". That's what's happening in the eastern part of the Congo.

As I said earlier, we have the wrong understanding of power. We think that we need to eliminate others to have control. Don't you need those people? Have you ever seen you own brother come against you? We know that our own family members may come against us, but then a stranger gives us water and comes to help us out. So, we don't even know who our family is. We don't understand our race. We base it on the color of our skin. People will come and tell you, "I have a Black friend", "I have a Hispanic friend", "I have a White friend." No! You have a friend, period. We have only one race: the human race. In the process, we are trying to kill each other.

I used to envy the US when I was in the Congo. I used to think, "Wow, what a nation!" In the US, you see people coming from all over. That is one thing that makes the strength of America—you have unique Americans: Asian Americans, African Americans, Caucasian Americans--people from all over the world and they are American. It doesn't matter how they speak because you will find different accents. America was the country that would embrace anybody, but, with all that I've seen, it's changing. I am not saying in that it's 100%, but I feel like America is taking the wrong direction. It's very dangerous.

What makes the power of America great is that you will find somebody here in America who speaks Tshiluba. The Congolese person who speaks Tshiluba is really someone who speaks with a dialect of the Congo, but here, he's an American. You see that person loving America with all his heart. He's an American, and he wants to serve his country. Because the US has people coming from all over, that's what makes America very strong.

For example, the naturalized Congolese Americans will defend America against the Congo because they believe they are Americans, not Congolese. They will stand up and defend America and release information and secrets about what the Congo wants to do against America because they are American. They're not Congolese, even though they speak the same language as the Congolese in Africa. I see people from Mexico,

Canada, China and other nations coming to the US who also join the army to defend their new country. On the other hand, maybe an American born and raised here betrays his own country. So, who is the real American—the American born and raised here who betrays his country or the stranger who becomes a naturalized US citizen and lays down his life to defend America?

I feel like America's losing it now; that is, losing its role on the world stage, and here is the reason why I am telling America all these things. I strongly believe that God's heart is in America. I'll say that these people are a people of God. That's why the enemy is fighting America in so many ways. He is wanting to destroy America because America plays a significant role in the world. These words are coming from my heart, and as you are reading this, I want you to pause, even for one minute, and pray for this nation. I want you to pray for the leaders of this nation. Don't fight them. Don't curse them. Pray for them. Pray that God will bring them together and they will be united again. There is a reason why the Founding Fathers called this nation the United States of America. So, I want you to pray for real unity among the leaders and pray that God will protect them and protect the future of this nation.

The entire world, not just America, has become very divided. You will see people thinking about creating weapons and wanting to have the most powerful one. If we've heard that another nation has a more powerful weapon, then we're concerned. If we see another nation with that weapon, then we think we must take it because we want to be in power. That is not power. Power is also bringing people together, trying to understand what they are thinking about, where they're coming from, and what they're believing, so that we can think about what we can do together as human beings. But, that's not us anymore. We just think about killing each other every day. It doesn't matter what we look like or how we talk. One nation. One people.

We have hurt each other in the past and even now. Do we want to keep hurting each other in the future? I believe you can be the key. Change doesn't take many people. Just one person, and it can be you, my reader! You can see how dark this world is, so take a minute and say a prayer. How many racially offensive words are out there? We can go search for them in the past, whether it's the n-word or the word cracker or the word Pocahontas— these words have hurt people. We don't want to stay in the past. We want to think of the future generations. What is the legacy we want for our children?

Here on earth, we are all strangers in one way or another. If you have never been a stranger, then it would be hard for you to treat a stranger with love. People who are out of their native countries should know how to treat a stranger because they know what it feels like. I interviewed Matt Holt who is the Vice President of Human Resources in the company where he and I work. He is one of the kindest people I know—very approachable and welcoming. Matt always has a smile on his face, includes others and doesn't look down on others. Here is the portion of his interview that I would like to share: "So, I studied abroad in Spain at the University of Valencia, I played rugby and went to school. I lived with a family who only spoke Spanish, so my Spanish got a lot better as I spoke it for survival. No one spoke English. From a language standpoint, it was very different. I felt different. I was an

American. I spoke English. I'm a big guy, you know, lots of reasons that I was different. One of the things that happened that made me feel more comfortable was on the rugby field. One day at practice, one of my teammates pointed at my shirt below my chin, and I looked down, and he smacked me. (Have you ever had anything like that happen to you?) And it made me realize that just like growing up in Chicago in the United States that we're all the same, you know, that people do the same silly jokes in Spain, and they're from another part of the world than from where I'm from. It really was like a big moment for me. We're all the same, even though we may look different, have different languages, and have different tastes, in our essence, we're all kind of the same."

Let's put our differences on the side and embrace our diversity as a gift. We don't want to be the same, otherwise, we'll have the same ideas. We want fresh ideas from China, from Australia, from the Congo, and from all over the world. Let's be one and let's share this same message with Congo, Uganda, and Rwanda. Let's not fight. Let's encourage one another and acknowledge other people's gifts. Bless them as much as you can, and that gift will be a blessing for many generations.

We're allowing this world to shepherd us and to give us the form it wants to. Today, we see women acting like the way the world wants them to act. We see men acting the way the world wants them to act. And children. And youth. We have all been sacrificed in a way. We're all angry. Women want to defend themselves because some men have taken advantage of them. Children want to take the place of their mothers or fathers and make their own rules. Parents used to spank their children, but if you spank them today, then they can call the police on you. So, today, the kids can tell the adults what to do. It's a very big confusion. Our human identity has taken on different forms on all levels. Today, you will see how people present themselves, how women present themselves, or how men present themselves—you will be ashamed and amazed.

Today, we live in a society that, when people are fighting each other, it's fun. We take our cameras and film them and post it, and it's fun. We might see someone getting beaten up on the street.

We just pull out our camera. We film it. It's fun. We see someone having a heart attack. It's fun. It's a Facebook world. I am not against all social media and things, but it's getting crazy. We don't communicate anymore with people, and we are too connected to machines. We have become so addicted to our phones that we don't talk to each other and a lot of families fall apart. You can have five people in the same room and it will be quiet because nobody is talking to each other. They're all connected to their cell phones. It's crazy and getting crazier. We humans have lost our way. We have lost our value and sense of family.

You see someone on the street. Someone can be struggling and it's so hard for us to reach out. It's so hard to say, "How are you?"—a simple phrase like that. Everyone is so busy in the world that we don't pay attention to what's happening in other people's worlds. We are concerned with ourselves and have become so selfish. It's all about us. That's who we've become. It's our identity. We have to find our way. We have to go back to where we used to be. We have to go to the place of caring, the place of accepting, the place of understanding and tolerance. We're all different in so many ways. We don't have to be the same.

One thing I love about my employer and one thing that they say is that they don't want to change you. They want you to share who you are. We all have different backgrounds, different stories, and different experiences. In order to live together with others, we have to understand where they're coming from. We need to understand their stories and let them share their stories. People behave the way they behave and there's always a reason behind it. But, if you don't let them share their stories and listen, then you're not going to understand the way they behave. What you basically do is judge them and put them to the side. So, we have lost our way as human beings.

We mustn't forget that every decision we make now will affect our future and the future of our children. Sometimes, I wonder if, because of the way we think and make decisions, our children will become machines. I am not against all the advances we are making in robotics and technology. We use them to make our lives easier, but it's not good if they are controlling us. Steve Jobs, co-founder of Apple, once said that the advances in AI could be dangerous for us. The danger is not the machine itself, but the danger is when we let it use us. We have to use computers, cell phones, and the like, but they don't have to use us.

It's easy for human beings to be controlled by something, whether it's money or machines or whatever. We let all these things use us. I believe that machines are already controlling us. We use machines to make our jobs easier. We use them to make our lives easier. The danger is that those machines will start using us. We wake and sleep with our phones. Some people use them for work. Some people live for computers. We know that technology can be good, but let's think now about our children. We are trying so many things that can be dangerous for our future. We are trying many things that can be very compromising to our children's future. We don't think about them, do we?

Today, we don't even know what manhood or womanhood is anymore. We have what society is telling us, and it's crazy. We have become more and more divided in terms of race and in terms of ethnicity, gender, and age. We're getting divided in terms of race, because every group wants to be in power, considering only how they believe and how they view things, and so we are divided. The more we disagree, the more we want to kill each other and it is crazy. We are falling apart!

We are heading toward a time when we will need each other immensely and we'll need each one of us to function in our role and in our calling. I ask you to think about it. There are things we cannot change, but let's just pray about it. Let's pray for the future of our children. I don't know if you're concerned, but I am concerned. I am concerned about the future. If you are concerned like me, then I want you to pause and pray. Pray for your children, grandchildren, great-grandchildren, and great-great-grandchildren. You won't know most of them, perhaps beyond your grandchildren or great-grandchildren, nor the struggles they will have, but you know the struggles facing our children now.

You know how hard it is to educate our children today. There are so many voices out there. Yesterday was easy, but today you're not the only one talking to them. You talk to your children, but there are all kinds of influences on them. There's what social media might tell them and what television might tell them. In school, they are told things and you might get upset about those things, but you cannot change that because they decided to give them that program. Our children hear all kinds of things in their own neighborhoods. I was shocked when I heard a story of an eight-year-old girl watching pornography. I don't know if this is something you would have brought to your parents when you're very young. Children are on their phones and some of our parents don't set up any rules and let them use their phones any way they want to use them. Children will be on their tablets or phones for the entire day and we don't do anything about it. That's where we are, and as a result, we're losing them. So, if it's this bad for our children, then how bad will it be with our grandchildren and great-grandchildren? We're not concerned about it, are we? Let's pray for them.

I agree that we do have some differences, such as the languages we speak and the way we look on the outside. On the inside, we are all the same. We cry the same way. We rejoice the same way.

We have the same bodily functions when we eat. We have the same bodily functions after we eat. In reality, we have the same blood. We are one people. We have one race. It's the human race. Let's be one. Let's be united.

Observe our history. If we go back in time, how many fallen kingdoms will we see? Why do you think they have fallen? Values, they lost their values.

We know Egypt used to be the most powerful nation in the world and it was in Africa. Look at Egypt today—they have lost it. Something must have gone wrong. We need to learn what that is. Today, the US can be number one, but something could go wrong and we could lose it all. We don't want that. We don't want that! The US has been a blessing to many countries.

The US has to be the mother of all these countries. We don't want to see our politicians fighting each other. We don't want to see our leaders criticizing each other and calling each other names. Oh no! What example do we get from that? What example do we give our children? So, for them, leading will be insulting each other and calling each other names. So what heritage

149

do you give us? And I know when I stand up here, people will say, "Who's this African guy giving us advice?" Wisdom is not based on where you come from, what you look like, what you have, or what you don't have. These are simple words, but these words, if you take them to heart, they will be a blessing, not only to you, but to many others. So, this is for every leader in the world: be an example to us. We're neither judging nor condemning, but encouraging you. There are so many beautiful things that you are doing. That's what we want. Let's put aside our differences. We don't want you to fight about unimportant things. You can fight with ideas. You can challenge each other with ideas, not insults. That's not the heritage we want.

This is for all the good police officers who want to make a difference. It is for all politicians with good morals and with good hearts who are fighting for a better future. It is for all good employers who are giving everyone an equal opportunity. This is for all who have put their lives on display to help our world become a better place. I encourage you to keep trying. Don't give up and don't get discouraged.

This is for all my Caucasian people who are frustrated and who want to make a difference for all the Black people who are being hurt in so many ways. Black lives matter and all lives matter. I will say it one more time. This is for all my Black people who have been hurt in so many ways. Black people matter, and all people matter.

I will say there's a lot of frustration today. Knowing that I am coming from a different nation, you might think that the violence there is worse. When I was in Congo, yes, I saw a lot of violence there. You can lose your life over your speech, you don't have rights, and there's oppression in Congo. It's everywhere we go. There's all kind of tension. Here in the US, there's a great deal of tension between the Black community and the White community. Why is there injustice? Why are the police shooting Black people? Tension is everywhere we go.

The problem here is not on the color of your skin. The world has become so evil. A bad heart is a bad heart, no matter what you look like. Some Black people have very dark hearts, but so do some White, Asian, and Hispanic people. It can be anyone. There are also nice people with good hearts all over the world. It's not based on the color of your skin. People can disagree on a lot of things. I don't have to agree with everything that everyone says. It can be the same in my family. We can still disagree. It means that we don't see things from the same perspective. Maybe from where I am standing, I see from the front and you see from the back and we will stand there arguing all day long and we don't find a solution.

I believe we're all concerned. I'm concerned. It's part of our identity. As human beings, we must be concerned and, if we are concerned, then let's work it out. We can do this! We can change this! It's possible. We must refuse to ignore unjust actions and harsh words that hurt. There are a lot of horrible things that have happened in our past. Let's leave those things behind us. We don't want to remind each other about slavery and colonization. We don't want to remind each other of genocide. We don't want to remind each other of the Holocaust and of the mass destruction of World War I and World War 2.

What are we doing in our past? We still live in it. We pretend to be so advanced, but we're not—we're still living in the past. Why do we want to go back to those dark places? It only brings more frustration. The minute we look at that darkness we think, "Let's just blow everything up. Blow it up!" Is that what you want? Is that what we want? I do not know. Why do you want to be a part of that? If you don't, then don't remain apathetic and silent. Do good. Refuse evil and make a change.

Sometimes, we think that change has to be major. We believe that we can't influence change unless we go on TV and talk about it or post it on social media. Sometimes, people don't even pay attention to those things. Change comes daily, whether it is at work with your coworker or whether it's at the restaurant with a stranger. Step up for things that are unjust. Stand up for injustice. Step up. Don't be afraid to speak up.

I like a story that my friend Loranda told me. She was at a restaurant and, after she and her family had finished eating, a young Hispanic man came up to her and asked, "Can I clean your table?" They were done, and Loranda was just sitting there, and he started cleaning. Then, his boss came up to him and started yelling at him, "No, Jose! No!" in a very rude and disrespectful manner. (I like how Loranda just stepped up.) She said, "No! No to you!" The boss was like, "What?", and Loranda said, "No to you, because he asked me if he could clean up." The boss started apologizing to her, and Loranda said, "No, no, no, no, no! Do not apologize to me. You need to apologize to this young man. You do not do that. Next time you want to give him feedback, make sure you take him to the back to speak with him. You do not do that in front of people." Acts of kindness like that are what we need to do every day. Do not treat people disrespectfully because of who they are. Do not treat people like that!

As I said earlier, I believe change can come from one person. I don't want to be judgmental. So, how can I help? How can you help? The most important thing is that, as humans, we don't like to admit that we've failed. We have failed. We are the ones causing the problem. Just like

_____

[6]https://www.brainyquote.com/quotes/albert_einstein_121993 Copyright © 2001 - 2018 BrainyQuote

Einstein said, "We cannot solve our problems with the same thinking we used when we created them[6]."

We caused the problem as human beings and sometimes it is bigger than us. We'll need someone who is higher to come and assist us because the problem we are causing is too hard for us to fix. We try. We have been united as a nation. What do you think? Did the idea of the United States work? The Founding Fathers let God be the center of everything.

In reality, we see everyone today coming with the mindset, "What can we get out of this?" It's not about what we are going to give. Do we come up with ideas as to how we are going to help the world, or do ask ourselves what are we going to get in return? It is tough. It's a difficult subject to talk about. Saying these things might get me into trouble because people don't want to hear it. They hide from the truth and don't want to stand up and speak out.

I want you to have the courage to speak out. When something is wrong, tell it the way it is. We're not attacking people, but we are attacking wrong actions. Instead, we are killing each other. I might be wrong about something, but don't kill me. Kill my wrongdoing. That's what we need to do. We shouldn't want to kill each other. Instead, we have to fight with ideas. I can't say enough about how much I am inspired by Dr. Martin Luther King, Jr. I really admire him. He fought with ideas and today his idea worked. He said he had a dream, and it became a reality in the US, but look at us now! We are trying to destroy that dream. Can that dream become yours today? I am not talking just about this nation, the US. I am talking about the entire world.

As human beings, one thing we need to do is to admit that we have failed. We need God to intervene here because, until we finally realize that we do need help, things will continue to become darker and darker. Here's what we can say, "I admit I have failed. Let's admit we have failed, but here's my hand. With a pure heart, don't look at me from the outside. I know I'm Black. I hold out my hand." The person next to you could be Yellow, and the person after him might be White. The person after you might look different, but let's hold each other's hands. We are one, so let's build a better future.

Don't stop the chain from growing. Hold the hand of the person next to you and ask that person to hold the hand of the person next to him. I know it will be tough. It will take some trust. It will take some patience. Let's keep seeking. Let's keep asking. It's possible. We can do it!

CHAPTER 9 FORGIVENESS

Pain hurts. It's hard to understand if you've never experienced it. It can come in different forms. It could be a stranger that hurt you, but then, you're like, this is a stranger. But what if it's someone that you know? What if it's someone that you trust? What if it comes in a way you will never expect? So, here the situation changes. The pain will be different depending on the who.

And here I am trying to talk about forgiveness. I have a case and God knows what it is. What about yours? Maybe someone betrayed you or cheated on you. This is not easy-- me coming and telling you that you have to forgive—but, it's for your good. This is a big risk that I'm taking. You may get mad at me, not like what I'm going to tell you, or you won't be open to hearing what I'm trying to tell you. We all have our own experiences.

Maybe you have been raped and the person who raped you is not a stranger, but your own father. I don't have the courage to tell you that you have to forgive him, but I will try. Maybe you have invested a lot in a relationship. You have given all you have—your money, your time, your heart, your mind and soul—and your partner betrayed you by taking it all and leaving with it. I am trying to imagine your pain and feel what you are feeling. I can only imagine how many times you have woken up at night crying, how many times you have felt like your heart was about to explode, the anguish in trying to explain your pain to people, but nobody understood—you were there by yourself, in pain, feeling felt like the world was ending. You were stuck, along with everything around you. Confusion was your friend. Depression was your master. There was no light at all. How many times have you prayed to die?

I am even talking about the young girl who lost her relationship with her mother because her stepfather raped her. She went and told her mother, but her mother didn't believe her and kicked her out of the house. She would cry out at night "Mom!", but her mother wasn't there. Out there in the cold, she was left alone in painful confusion. Then there is the young man in Africa who was kicked out of his home because his family said that he was a witch. He didn't even know what a witch was, but he was told to get out. His family had singled him out, blaming him for all the chaos in the house. They said he was the reason why his father lost his job and he was confused. He was cast out and had to learn to survive on his own...painful.

Trust me, it is not easy for me to come here and tell you that you have to forgive. Like me, you trusted this person, but this person took away your trust. He took what was valuable to you. He took your identity and forgiveness is part of your identity. It is part of our identity and is the most powerful thing in the world to have, yet hard to apply.

On the day that this person hurt you, he put you in a prison called Hate and Anger and you don't want to forgive. But, when you don't want to forgive, then you put yourself in solitary confinement. Think again about Nelson Mandela. He wanted to free these people and it caused him a lot of pain. He went to prison where they treated him like a criminal, but he refused to be a captive. The person who put him in prison thought he had him, but Mandela was a free man, and I'll tell you why—there was no hate in his heart. Had he hated the person who did that to him, he would have felt like he was in solitary confinement, but he refused that. He was a free man because he forgave and stopped a lot of bloodshed during the time of Apartheid.

Nelson Mandela could have come out of prison saying, "You know what, South Africa, revenge!", which would have only led to more violence and killing. Instead, he came out of prison with forgiveness, stopped the bloodshed, and said that we as a people needed to forgive. They didn't understand him. South Africa developed more than any other African country during that time. Why? This wise man chose to forgive his captors. Was it easy? No! Because of what he went through, he lost his wife and his family fell apart.

This man knew about pain, but because he could forgive, he had power over the person who hurt him. One thing we don't realize is that the person who hurt you is trying to have power over you. When you fight that with force, anger, and hatred, you give that person the power that he wanted. This is what I am trying to say here. You are a nice person. You are a kind person. You are a sweet person, but you've lost that because somebody hurt you. Is that your true identity or do you have the identity that someone has given you?

Once, I read a story about a South African man who had murderers come to his house and shoot his mother and father. He was so angry that he took a gun, went and hunted them down, and killed them. After that, he became a killer, but he wasn't a killer before that day—he became one because someone gave him that identity. The minute they murdered his parents, he allowed anger and hate to take over, so that became his identity. Once it became his identity, that same identity drove him to that behavior. This same man was once a good boy who lived at home and listened to what his parents told him. Yet, today when his aunts and uncles try to tell him that, he won't listen to them. He says, "I am a killer. That's who I am." In reality, it's not.

Also, how many girls have given up on guys because they have been hurt by a guy who they loved and trusted? Since this guy hurt them, they think, "You know what? We will never trust men again!" As a result, one of those girls will try having a relationship with other girls like her who don't trust men. She wants to be in a relationship, but because a guy has hurt her, she thinks it won't work. On the other hand, maybe you're a guy who was abused by your own father, who told you that you're not a man. Every day, your father told you that while beating and abusing you, then you started believing that, so your father gave you that identity.

Others might be out there who you haven't experienced this chaos. We cannot say that this pain is greater than that one. We all react differently given the situation. One situation can be tough and then get easier, or it can be easier and then become tougher. Pain is pain, so I cannot take your pain for granted.

What I want you to do is to go back and compare the person you were to who you are now. Maybe you started drinking, not because you enjoyed it, but to numb the pain. In the process, you became an alcoholic. The same thing happens with drugs. You started doing drugs to forget about what has happened and now you are addicted. Then, when you're sober, the pain has actually doubled. The reality is that you are in pain. Don't avoid or hide it, confront it. There's a way out — look forward.

You hurt because you're still living in the past--in that moment when that person

163

hurt you and stole what was most valuable to you. You need to realize that today is a new day. The horrible thing that happened is way back there. Don't feel discouraged. There's a power within you! You are free to take it back and say, "I am going to live a better life now and tomorrow and into the future". Yes, there was damage. Trust me, I believe you and I know that you suffered damage, but do know what will cause more damage? Allowing that pain to take over and not seeing that those days and that person are gone. Think of how many people you've lost and what've you've lost because of pain. This pain has caused you to lose your job and push people who love you away—all because you were angry. Trust me, I know you have the right to be angry. I'm angry, too, but what I don't want you to do is to allow that anger to take control of you. You don't want that.

I shared my story in an earlier chapter and it was like yours. There was no one with whom I could share what was happening. I didn't tell anyone what my stepmother was doing to me. I couldn't tell my father nor my mother. I was in pain, so as I grew up, I started seeking revenge. The more I didn't see it happen, the more I became angry. I would seek revenge to the point where I wished that person dead. When it didn't happen, I became angrier. I became violent and an alcoholic, but inside there was a sweet boy in a prison. Deep inside there was a person ready to love. I had so much love but I couldn't release it because I was in prison. And remember, when you are in prison, you can't buy or sell, you don't have anything, nor do you have your own identity.

It's the same thing with unforgiveness. You can't think about anything else because it consumes your mind. Even if you have great things happening in your present, you don't think about them. You are stuck in the past, and as a result, you cannot plan for the future. Your sole focus is on that person who hurt you. You want that person to see you succeed, yet you cannot move forward because you are trapped in the past.

All the greatest stories of the world have been shaped by forgiveness—Martin Luther King, Jr. Nelson Mandela. Christ. A dear friend of mine, Pastor Kendahl, also has a story about forgiveness. Kendahl, his wife, and his children moved into the home of his spiritual father and his wife to join his church and serve with him. There was no money that drew Kendahl to come and work for his spiritual father's ministry. He was passionate about serving God and helping people, and God used him powerfully in this church. He and his family loved the pastor and his wife and happily worked side-by-side with them. Then one day, Kendahl was blindsided by a betrayal by two people he trusted the most: his spiritual father and his wife. The pain was so devastating that he could barely eat. He couldn't go to work without weeping. He was consumed by the painful thoughts of this betrayal and the ones who hurt him.

Can you imagine how hard it was for him? He would come home from work, stay in his own little box, and suffer in pain. He had lost everything: his job, his ministry, the support from his church family, his home, and his wife. It was hard for him to come out of the pain. He knew that his only way out of this prison he was in was to forgive. My friend shared with me that the pastor who betrayed him reached out to him in fear of revenge. This is what he said: "And while on the phone with him, my heart just broke. I somehow found myself trying to encourage him through this scenario. I felt somewhat foolish because I was so hurt and distraught and in despair that I couldn't eat, I couldn't sleep, I couldn't function at work, and here I am, attempting to let the man that has hurt me very deeply know that I won't be seeking vengeance because Jesus is my example, and as Jesus looked into the faces of those who had judged Him falsely, treated Him wrongly, and even took pleasure in His pain, He looked to them and said, 'Father, forgive them, because they don't know what they're doing" And somehow, some way, by the power of the Holy Ghost, I was able to speak to the man that probably was a part of the greatest pain I had ever experienced, and forgive him by the Word of God, just by acting on the Word."

Looking at Kendahl's story, I think it's amazing how he came out of his pain—Kendahl knew that forgiveness was the key. He said, "Until we can allow through the Word of God to receive the forgiveness that Christ has already purchased and then to release it into other people's lives, it is then and only then that we will begin to encounter the authority of the

Word, the intimacy and the communion of the Holy Spirit, and through releasing the offense that takes place in this world, in this life, in the realm of time, we make ourselves available to the Holy Spirit to take us into the realm of the Spirit and begin to manifest the kingdom of Heaven in the earth." Because he has experienced the freedom of forgiveness, he and his new wife are working toward building a better future.

Today, we live in a society that teaches an eye for an eye—if you hurt me, then I will hurt you. That's how it is, but we forget that forgiveness plays a significant role in our identity. What you will do tomorrow depends on it. What you don't realize is that the minute that you get mad or hate somebody, you lock yourself into a prison. You can't think straight anymore and all you think about is your time of revenge. It consumes you, but the minute you forgive, you start thinking clearly again. When you can think straight, you can ask yourself important questions, such as: What can I do better? What can I do differently? How can I understand why the enemy is attacking me?" In order to heal the person that has hurt you, you must first forgive him. What we don't realize is that the person who hurt you might hurt more people. The only way of saving that person is by setting him free—setting his spirit free—through the power of forgiveness.

I have experienced that myself. I've been hurt a lot in my past. I grew up with the thought of 'This is not fair! This person has to pay! And, because this person cannot put a price of what he did to me, he hurt me again. It hurt me even more." I was in this prison, seeking revenge. I wanted this person to pay! The more he didn't pay, the more I felt hurt.

When I was a child in the Congo, I was supposed to take malaria medicine, but I refused to because the pills were so bitter. I compare this to forgiveness—it is difficult to swallow like bitter medicine. You are mad and afraid, and you don't want to swallow the pill, yet you have to swallow that pill to stay healthy. You will have drink forgiveness to be free.

My freedom came by forgiving this person who hurt me. Soon, the things that were consuming my mind and my heart were gone. I knew that I had completely forgiven this person by the way I was able to pray for him. I was free to think about myself, my life, and my future. But in that prison, I could do nothing.

The scar that you have on your chest or on your heart is a gift—one that the Enemy has given you that will hurt you. You might want to argue with me right now and say, "Well, how can you call it a gift?" Well, look at you now—you have become wiser, more passionate, humbler, and more cautious. Where did you get it from? What we don't realize is this: what caused our pain yesterday can be a blessing tomorrow and that same pain can be a blessing to many people.

Like you, I have been hurt so bad. I know what you're going through. I know and can feel your pain, but that pain has become a gift. Today, my experiences give me enough words to come and encourage you. The words that I have are from an experience—a very bad experience, a place of darkness. To come out of that place, I had to forgive. Forgiveness gave me the power to live my present better and to look to the future. Hate locked me in a cell, and all I wanted was revenge, but that wasn't the way.

I understand now what Joseph meant to his brothers. His brothers sold him as a slave. Psalm 105:17 explains that it wasn't his brothers' plan. God allowed it and caused it to happen because what He had planned for Joseph was bigger. God had a great plan, but, first Joseph had to be sold as a slave. That was a very bad process and he didn't deserve it.

You don't deserve to go through what you're going through--to be raped, abused, beaten up, or cheated on. You did everything you could possibly do for this person, but in return, he hurt you. Listen to me: there is a good purpose behind what you're going through. Look at what Joseph told his brothers, "What you did to hurt me, God transformed it to good. Now, I am a blessing to you." The very person they sold into slavery delivered them! And I know, you might be the Joseph who doesn't want to give his brother a chance, but you must. In order to enjoy what God has for you, you have to release that person from your heart, let it go, and forgive. If you focus on the shame, bad words, and abuses…if you focus on them, then you will not be able to forgive. You have to minimize it. You have to be on top of it. You have to be more powerful than it. You can do it. It is possible, but you have to want to do it.

Nelson Mandela could have responded through anger, but decided not to. He was already in prison. He worked for freedom because he chose to forgive those who hurt him. He saved a lot of people after him—his nation and his people—but he had to forgive first. What you don't realize is that, the minute you forgive, many people will enjoy freedom after you. By forgiving your husband, who cheated on you, you will save your children. By saving your children, you will save generation after generation.

By forgiving that one person, you will go out there, tell your story and your testimony will save a lot of people. Sometimes, we present the bad that people do to us, and we wait for it to transform people's lives. No! It's about your forgiveness. When the people see what you did, they will be like, "Where does she get that power to forgive?" And your story will inspire a lot of people.

Forgiveness is where you start. Why are we shaken by Christ? He forgives people. He doesn't hurt them. He started by forgiving them and that's where the transformation happens. The ones who hurt you already know what they've done. You don't have to remind them, "You're a rapist" and 'You're a killer." They already know it. In order for them to be able to come out, it's only by that power of forgiveness and you are the key. If you don't set them free, they'll continue doing the same thing—and you know that you don't want them to go and hurt other people.

Unforgiveness causes us to live in the past. We have all experienced that in a way, but there's hope because life has a lot to give you and you can still move forward. By forgiving that person, you gain your freedom. Nelson Mandela didn't want to live in the past by thinking about those who hurt him. Instead, he wanted to move forward by forgiving them. Unforgiveness is a chain that keeps you bound, making it hard for you to move, think, or plan for the future. You can't move forward, and you still want revenge because you are hurt. And the more you don't see revenge happening, the more it hurts you, and the more you are unable to do anything.

Forgiving is a very hard deal. You have people who tell you, "Just forgive this person!" Well, you know what it's like once you've experienced it--it's hard! Remember the friend whom I was helping—the one who had an issue, didn't have a car, or a good job? I have another story to tell you.

A friend whom I was pastoring needed a car and I wanted to help him. Many of you would say that it was a poor decision. We all make poor decisions and know the reason why we make them. We often make a fool of ourselves because we love and trust people. He needed a car and I cosigned for him to get it. In order for him to pay for the car, he needed a better job, so I helped him get one. When the company sent me a bill for eleven thousand dollars, telling me this is what he owed for the car, I realized what had happened…again. I won't lie, it hurt.

On the day I got the bill, I went to him and told him that I didn't have that money, but he refused to help me with it. Again, I felt hurt and betrayed. I didn't have that money and I had other bills. I asked the car company to work with me and set up a payment plan because I didn't have that much money. During this time, I had to preach on forgiveness. God confronted me with this: "Can you forgive this man?" I went back and forth, and the Lord asked me to put a price on his soul. God asked me how much this man was worth—eleven thousand dollars? God told me that no one else will give him a chance, so He wanted me to and to trust him. It was hard, but I knew I had to let it go and forgive him. This bill has been paid off and I don't owe any more money.

I don't know how it happened, because I didn't have enough money. Somehow, I was able to pay it off, and that was amazing. Had I acted and reacted differently, this man would have given me a different identity and I would have continued to make other poor decisions. Yes, he hurt me, but I have learned something—what he did to hurt me became a blessing to me. The person who hurt you actually blessed you! You may disagree with me. If you look at it the situation differently, then you will see that you have become wiser, stronger, more aware, and can help a lot of people. It's like what I said with Nelson Mandela. There was already a lot of bloodshed, but he came out of prison and stopped it by forgiving. Had he not forgiven, then there would have been more bloodshed—an eye for an eye.

People who have come out of painful situations are able to help a lot of people because they've become wiser through that experience. What happened to me in the past— the pain and the abuse—helped me to become a stronger person. All these experiences have built my character.

Another person you must forgive is yourself. Sometimes, you blame yourself and say this is your fault. I have thought the same thing. A victim of rape may blame herself because of the way she was dressed or that she seduced him. No, it isn't your fault. You didn't do anything to deserve what happened to you. Trust me, it is not your fault. It's on the person who took what was valuable to you. Don't ever think that you are weak. The person who came to attack you is weak. You must be stronger, and in presenting your true character, you can help   that person find himself.

Forgiveness transforms lives. It's not only going to transform your life, but also the lives of the people around you and in your family. People are out there waiting to hear your story. For you to have the courage to go and tell that story, you need first to forgive and be in a position of power or you will only be presenting your pain. Once you present your pain, tell us that your pain is in the past. You have to come out and tell people that it's possible. You might be saying, "No, I don't want to forgive him! No, that person is the devil. That person destroyed me. That person killed me." Are you really dead? Is that the person you want to be? Have you been destroyed? Change that! You are not destroyed! Put yourself back together and stand up! You can do it! You have a lot to give and there is a lot in your story. You have a power within you—don't take it for granted.

That power is the simple decision to say "I forgive you. I forgive myself. It's all over. It's all in the past! I want to live out my days and go to my bright future." Nelson Mandela impacted many generations because he forgave. Christ impacted the world because He forgave. Forgiveness is not for people who deserve it—it's for people who don't. It is tough, but you have that power in you...make that decision now. I know you are looking back at all of the things that have happened to you and might even be in tears now. Forgiveness is still possible. If I did it, Christ did it, and countless other men and women did it, then you can do it. It's not, never has it ever been, nor will it be easy. That's why it's for the tough. It's possible for the tough ones like you. You are strong. So, break those chains and come out as a free man and go free other people like you.

CHAPTER 10 MY IDENTITY

Who am I? I have asked myself this question a lot. Growing up, I went in so many different directions trying to find myself. In an earlier chapter, I talked about how I got lost in the process. You won't believe this, but the one thing that helped me to find myself was a dream that I had.

When I was little, I was surrounded by abuse and violence—my father raising his hand against my mother and my stepmother abusing me. I didn't know who I was. There was a lot of confusion in that little boy's mind. As I said in Chapter 2, I was a lonely child—depressed, worried, and so scared. During the chaos I was living in, I had a dream where I was playing with a man—a stranger. I felt so peaceful and I had never felt that peace in real life. I was having fun playing with him. I won't try to describe His physical features, but only focus on the fact that man in my dream had the character and personality of a good father.

He was kind and concerned more about me than about anything else. I never had the kind of attention nor love this man was giving me. I had never felt any of this before. He cared me in a way that no other person had ever cared for me. Then, he told me when it was time for him to go. I told him that I wanted to go with him, but he said that it wasn't the right moment. When I woke up, I was sad because the person who I was looking for was gone.

As time passed, I felt lost. I had a hole in my heart. I tried everything, but nothing could fulfill that emptiness in my heart. I didn't believe in anything. I was empty, angry, desperate, and suicidal. As I was about to end my life, that dream was the only thing that gave me hope. That dream was real to me, so I needed to dig in and to search. It helped me and gave me a reason to try one more time to challenge the Man in my dream.

To me, that person in my dream was Christ. Based on what I had been taught in school or in church, but, in my soul, I thought," No, Christ is a made-up story. No! People created the story of Christ just to control us, and I don't believe." I remember saying these words, "If you do exist, you better show up now. I don't believe in you," I was bold! "I don't believe in you. I don't believe that you exist, but if you do, show up!" The only thing I had—there was no pastor or anybody around me—was a Bible. (I still have that Bible today. Even though I can buy myself any Bible, I like this Bible, because it was the tool that helped me find myself.)

I began reading and searching the Bible but finding nothing. I would dig and dig and read and read, but nothing made sense. I was reading and talking to Someone Who I didn't believe in. I read through different books. I remember reading Exodus and seeing that, if people did certain things, they would be punished. I remember closing that book shut and thinking to myself, "This is why people don't believe. If You do exist, then why does there have to be violence and so much chaos?" I got mad, closed my Bible, and asked why. I still remember the answer that came to me: "If you never experience the darkness, then light won't make sense to you."

Believe me, all these questions you have, I have them too. Why is there so much suffering? Why do people have to die? You might say, "I don't care. The world is evil," and you drop it right there. Yet, I chose to pray and read the Bible. My prayers were bold. When I was reading the Bible and I couldn't understand what I was reading I would say, "See! You're not real! You're not there!" Until one day, BOOM!

I had questions like everybody else: Who was this Christ? Was He real? Does He exist? Did He exist here on earth? Was He for real? Is He just a character in a made-up story? We have many answers from many different sources, but the decision to believe or not is on us. Through my research, I have discovered that many people recognize the existence of Christ. I am going to quote from one historical figure and what he had to say about Christ. Then, the decision to believe or not is yours. Albert Einstein said, "I am a Jew, but I am enthralled by the luminous figure of the Nazarene. Jesus is too colossal for the pen of phrase-mongers, however artful." He further added: "No man can read the Gospels without feeling the actual presence of Jesus. His personality pulsates in every word. No myth is filled with such life. Theseus and other heroes of his type lack the authentic vitality of Jesus.[7]" So, this experience that Einstein was talking about was what I had. All I had was the Gospels. Einstein was talking about the authenticity of Christ.

---

[7]http://smartandrelentless.com/find-out-what-these-famous-history-makers-had-to-say-about-jesus-christ/

You can read the Gospels from 2000 years ago and it still applies to men and women today. That is what Einstein was saying.

I found myself imitating as well. We grow up imitating what we see around us because society changes us. If we look back at ourselves eight years from now, we will not be the same. The children born will not look like us. Like a chameleon, we are trying to find the right color. We are not born to be rapists, thieves or murderers. Growing up around violence, I thought that was what I was supposed to do. I thought that, when I grew up, if others pushed me that I would push back. I was a chameleon. I didn't know who I was. I was still trying to find my identity.

Since my family was religious, I started imitating religion. Later on, I realized that there has to be more, so I gave up on that. I don't believe religion was what I was looking for. I was raised Catholic—they said God was my Father and gave me a set of beads to pray to Him. I didn't know who He was and wasn't connecting to Him. When I was in primary school I was Catholic, but I was raised Mormon.

In the process of finding yourself, you may be trying to imitate your friend, your father, your mother or society. You will still find something missing or feel that something that isn't right, but you keep on trying. Let me try. I tried with my father. Although he was a good person, there were still some areas that weren't right. What happens when a friend betrays you or isn't there for you? Is that the kind of person that you want to be? There's still something missing.

You are trying to search for it, maybe in society, but there's still something missing. We try with nature, but sometimes nature gets mad and pushes us back. We all search, but there remains a hole in our hearts. We're trying to find ourselves. We're trying to dig for it. We're trying to be who we see. Sometimes, it's by listening or observing, but still, we find nothing. So, we push and then become extremely frustrated. We have so many questions, but we can't find answers. We go to other people and ask, but they don't have the right answers.

Soon, I started imitating Christ and it was hard. By imitating Him, I had to forgive and that was the toughest part. I saw this Man going to the cross for people who treated Him like He was nothing. He didn't deserve to, but He did it anyway. Then, I saw aspects of His love—His unconditional love—that He was giving to people who didn't deserve it. And I began to really wonder, did anyone deserve it? No, but He did it anyway. I saw in His nature—simplicity, humility, encouraging others, and giving others hope. Seeing all these things, I thought, "This is who I want to be. I want to like Christ. I want to be able to forgive even those who don't deserve it. I want to love, not only people who deserve that love, but also to give that love unconditionally. I wanted to be able to save and give hope to others. This is who I want to be. I want to be Christ." I became attracted to that nature of His, to that love of His. He came into my heart and told me that the love He gave me, "I need you to go out and give it to someone who needs it." So, I fell in love with Him. The more I love, the more I fall in love, and, the more that love comes in, the more that love goes out. I want to be able to give that love.

My Christ, well, He's the only One Who set me free from depression, anger, and worry. I used to be scared, but all I had to do was allow

Him to come in. He took it all. He took all my pain and cries. He took my crisis. All I had to do was to allow Him to come in. All the emptiness in me... I used to think that I wasn't good enough. I believed that I wasn't intelligent. I didn't believe that I was able to write. All the voices...all the voices of negativity in my head—all the voices of the enemy telling me that it was over for me, that I was done, that I was nobody. The voices of people who used to tell me that I was nothing and wouldn't achieve anything. One of my favorite verses is Zechariah 4:6 ESV: "Then he said to me, 'This is the word of the Lord to Zerubbabel: 'Not by might, nor by power, but by My Spirit,' says the Lord of hosts." Lord, I need Your Spirit. I need You to come into me.

Now, He and I have become one. He lives in me and leads my life. He talks better than I do, so I let Him talk. If I have to write, He writes better than I do, so I let Him write. If I have to counsel somebody, then I allow Him to speak through me. If He asks me to forgive, He does it better than I do, so I allow Him to forgive people, even in things that are hard to forgive. But, once I allow Him to, He comes in and forgives. I don't question when He makes a decision. I let Him decide. He does it better than I do. He loves better than I do, and sometimes when I allow Him to love people through me, sometimes people get confused. This love is not my own. It belongs to somebody else. It is the most amazing love that you will ever imagine. I have never been loved that way by anyone else.

I remember the first day I accepted that love—I went crazy. I was giving things away like crazy. I was giving my clothes away—whatever I had. I thought I was crazy! I mean nothing else mattered. The world didn't matter to me. I thought that what I was looking for was success in this world, or friendship, or relationship. It wasn't that. I was looking for my identity. He is my identity. Nothing else mattered to me. I was like, "If this isn't Your kingdom, then take me. Take me there. Let's go." Then He told me, "There are other people like you here to love, so let's go out there and love as many people as we can."

Most of us we don't experience the fullness of His power or the fullness of transformation because we count Christ as a form of religion. He is not a religion. Christ was against all of these religious people who were like:" Do this. Do that. Don't do this. Don't do that." No! He is more about the relationship. He came to relate with people one-on-one. He was all about relationship. I'll give you an example. Marriage is a relationship. If your spouse is in the living room and you are in the bedroom, then you don't experience a marriage. The marriage is about the bedroom—the place of intimacy. It's an image of Christ.

For those of you who have read the Old Testament, you've read that the Temple has three parts. The first part is The Court—the Holy Place and the Holy of Holies. In the Holy of Holies, the priest would go there once a year—one priest. The Bible said that, once Christ came, He opened the Holy of Holies for us all, but remember that it was a place for one person. Christ has called us to be His bride. It's a picture of intimacy. Christ allows us to get married and experience that intimacy so that we can understand how deep our relationship is with Him. It's very deep. The intimacy between a man and a woman is very deep.

Some of us stay in the living room with Christ. We don't fully want Him. It stops us from experiencing the beauty. Actually, Christ is waiting for us in the bedroom. I decided to go in there, to go deeper, to find Him and experience Him in the fullness of who He is, and I fell in love and that loves burns in my chest every day. I always seek more. I always want more of Him. I am never content. I always want more. I want more of Him and I can't wait to see Him face-to-face. I love the Person, the Character of Christ.

I have a very good and dear friend of mine named Brenda. She is Catholic and, from time to time, I pray with her. She will often tell me, "Oscar, you need to try to interact with Mary." I have many, many friends who will tell me you need to try St. Paul or St. Peter, but there's one thing I need for them to understand. My relationship with Christ is so deep that it's impossible for me to bring anybody else into it. I cannot even allow my father to be involved in it. I cannot even have my best friend come into it. I cannot even have my pastor come into it. It's just that deep.

A good example I can share is that when a lion is having intimacy with a lioness, it is so dangerous that if you come and try to separate them, then the lion will kill you. The relationship with Christ is just like when you get married—the pastor will marry you guys, but will never go on the honeymoon with you. If you bring your pastor, even though he's a man of God, it's not going to work. You cannot even bring your best friend with you on your honeymoon—it's a place for you and your spouse. It's a place where only you two can be. That's the picture of Christ. It's just me and Him.

You know that what people experience on the outside they have already experienced on the inside. We see a lot of marriages, and we can appreciate what's happening on the inside. If the place of intimacy doesn't work, we see the result on the outside—one of which is divorce. Another result is fighting, but the real reason is that if the place of intimacy doesn't work, then the marriage won't work at all. So, that's the key right there.

Our relationship with Christ is not what we tell people. It's not when we go out there and say, "I love Christ." It's what people see. People will come to realize that there is something about this person. There's something happening. There's something going on. When people who are close to me see something different, it's only the result of what's happening inside—in the secret place—in a place of intimacy with Christ. That's what Christ did for me.

Christ gave me what my father wasn't able to give me. Christ gave me what my friend wasn't able to give to me. He gave what my mother couldn't give me. He gave what society and the world couldn't give me. He gave me what diplomas will never give me. He gave me what money doesn't give— the things you cannot receive.

Once, when I was in Texas, I was trying to encourage a homeless man. This homeless man started talking to me about Christ and told me what I wasn't able to tell him. What he told me was so powerful that it shook me. On my way home, I started thinking about how I would go to sleep in a bedroom on a bed, but what happened to this guy? How can this guy tell me about Christ? This is impossible! That's what Christ does to people! He gives you something that the world cannot give you.

This man, according to us, is on the streets, so how come he has peace? Many times, you think that you receive your peace from money, from a good job, from a relationship, but then you try it. You think, "Okay, maybe I'll be better if I get married", but then, you get married and you don't have it. "Okay, then maybe if I start having children," then, you start having children, and you don't have peace. You keep searching for happiness through a job promotion and you work harder and harder for more money and, when you get more money, you still have nothing. I have seen rich people with a lot of money—and my biological father was one of those people—who are empty inside. That's why I went to Christ. He gave me a friendship that nobody else could have ever given me. He will never release the secrets of my heart. I opened up to Christ. Some of us will open up to man—that's how we get deceived.

I open up to Christ and tell Him everything. I have nothing to hide from Him. He will never go out there and share our secret. The reason why it's Christ is that He will never judge me. He never judged me. He gave me a chance to be a better man by trusting Him, by following His lead and letting Him show me the way, and by copying whatever He did. That's why people come and say, "Well, at least you have something to give", and that's because everything I do, I have stolen from someone else, and that's Christ.

That's the kind of Friend we need. Listen, you can be friends with Donald Trump or the richest person on earth. You know what? You can be friends with the President, and you'll be happy for one term and perhaps a second term, but then it's gone. Maybe you'll be friends with a king, but he will pass away. You can rely on your father, but one day he'll be gone. You can rely on your money and keep looking at your bank account. Even the most powerful countries go down and the biggest economies crash.

If you rely on your money, know that you can lose it. If you rely on your friend because he's rich or a president or a king, know that he will pass away one day. Don't rely on people or things that are temporary. The reason why is that Christ is eternal. If I need counseling, He is the best counselor I could ever find. If I need comfort, He has the best words for me. If I want money, He has all the riches that I could ever imagine. That's why I pick Christ. He is powerful and all-knowing. That's why it's Christ. I'd rather rely on Him than my knowledge. I'd rather rely on him than my money. I'd rather rely on Him than my friends. I'd rather rely on Him than my family. The reason why is that Christ is not on His throne for one term or two terms. He's there for eternity. So even though you can come and say, "Oscar, wait until Christ's term is over." I'll tell you that it will never happen. Christ is there for eternity. That is why He is my identity.

Made in the USA
Columbia, SC
08 November 2024

45894765R00107